Endorsements

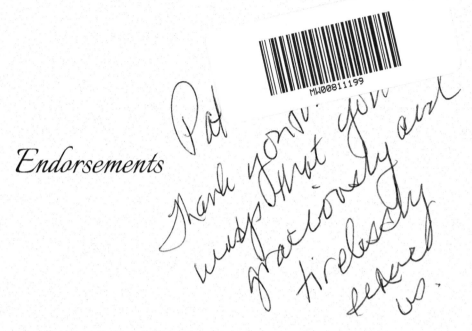

MILEPOST 95 IS BEAUTIFULLY written, touching, hope filled. Page takes you with her to the dark and scary places-constantly pointing to the only hope-God our Father. Masterfully written.

—Jami Amerine,
Author of *Stolen Jesus* and blogger at
Sacred Ground, Sticky Floors

ARE YOU AT ROCK bottom and wondering if God actually exists? I invite you to follow Page's journey to usher in hope to those places of your life that feel utterly hopeless. Watch as God unfolds in her life. Milepost 95 will help you regain trust that He can work in your life too.

—Carey Bailey
Life Coach
www.careybailey.com

MILEPOST 95

From Wreckage
to Redemption

MILEPOST 95

*From Wreckage
to Redemption*

PAGE GESKE

Published by Redemption Press, PO Box 427, Enumclaw, WA 98022

Toll Free (844) 2REDEEM (273-3336)

Redemption Press is honored to present this title in partnership with the author. The views expressed or implied in this work are those of the author. Redemption Press provides our imprint seal representing design excellence, creative content, and high quality production.

All Scripture quotations, unless otherwise indicated, are taken from the *Holy Bible, New International Version®*. NIV®. Copyright © 1973, 1978, 1984 by International Bible Society. Used by permission of Zondervan. All rights reserved.

Acknowledgments:
Holley Gerth, *You're Made for a God-Sized Dream: Opening the Door to All God Has for You*. Copyright © 2013 Baker Publishing Group, Ada, Mich.

John Eldridge, *Wild at Heart*. Copyright @2009 Thomas Nelson. Nashville, Tn.

Carol Hamblet Adams, *My Beautiful Broken Shell: Words of Hope to Refresh the Soul*. Copyright © 1998 Harvest House Publishers, Eugene, Ore.

Kevin Leman, *The Birth Order Book: Why You Are the Way You Are*. Copyright © 1982 Baker Publishing Group, Ada, Mich.

ISBN 13: 978-1-68314-575-2 (Paperback)
978-1-68314-576-9 (ePub)
978-1-68314-577-6 (Mobi)

Library of Congress Catalog Card Number: 2018930274

Contents

Dedication

TO MY MANY FRIENDS and family who encouraged me to tell my story, to keep writing, and *not give up on my God-sized dream*—because everyone's story matters.

But, especially to Holley Gerth, whose words helped me pursue my dream to write my story to encourage others to press on during difficult times. As I carried a copy of this quote around with me when I wrote in Barnes & Noble and other coffee shops, her words below helped me continue during the six years of writing this manuscript.

> At some point in pursuing your dream, you will get tired. You will sit down on the side of the road and say, "For crying out loud, if I knew it was going to be this hard and take this long, I never would have started down this path." Your job in those moments is simply this: don't quit. Because just over the next hill, just around the next bend is the breakthrough you've been waiting for, and you will miss it if you stop now . . . What's most likely to defeat you isn't external circumstances or challenges, it's you! Don't give into discouragement, doubt, or fear. Don't let the enemy tell you that you've goofed this

up for good and it's over. Just keep going. You will get there, one way or another.

—Holley Gerth
You're Made for a God-Sized Dream:
Opening the Door to All God Has for You

If you have a God-sized dream, pursue it with a vengeance and allow the Lord to bless you on the journey of seeking Him and His best for you with your whole heart.

Introduction

MILEPOST 95 IS MY story. The one I carry in my body that only I am qualified to tell.

It is a transparent story of the breaking of my protective shell through disappointments, a life-altering accident, emotional abandonment, major illness, and loss. Yet it is the story of perseverance, leaning into God, and learning to choose joy.

It is a story of the mileposts that have marked the major passages God has brought me through. The mileposts mark my journey in learning to trust, finding motivation to thrive, staying positive, and laughing through the storms and trials.

My story reveals how Jesus called me to be a light during a time of darkness and encouraging during a time of despair. And how He used a time of rehabilitation to bring me closer to Him while fulfilling the destiny that He had chosen for me.

If you are struggling with an unexpected and unwanted transition in your life, *Milepost 95* will remind you how God can use your most broken moments to give inspiration and hope to those around you. My story shows how Christ can take the wreckage of our lives, and redeem and transform it into a beautiful tapestry.

Two Final Prayers

Even though I walk through the darkest valley, I will fear no evil, for you are with me; your rod and your staff, they comfort me.

—Psalm 23:4

I LOOKED OVER AT my daughter Andrea at the wheel. The evening sun burnished her red hair with golden highlights that warm, summer evening. Taking a break from driving, I glanced out the passenger side window at the high desert flat terrain of eastern Idaho with its sagebrush and patches of lava rock.

She's doing great. Andrea was sixteen and enjoying driving our new-to-us Honda Pilot. I had driven most of the way from Kalispell, Montana. Andrea and I had a great road trip, talking and reflecting on the week behind us and before us.

I leaned my head on the window and smiled at the memories we had made in our week of family vacation in the Flathead Valley of Montana, near the majestic mountains of Glacier National Park.

After stopping at the Frontier Pie Shoppe restaurant between Idaho Falls and Blackfoot on Interstate 15, I had asked, "Would you like to drive?"

"Sure, Mom." Her face lit up. Andrea was always up for driving.

We had three hours to go before we'd be home. Andrea was a good driver. *This will be a great mother/daughter trust moment when I can show I believe in her driving abilities. It'll build her self-confidence.*

In the passenger's seat, I pulled out my thank-you notes and pen and worked on several notes. I had interviewed for several jobs in Montana before we left and wanted to get the notes checked off my to-do list before returning to work the next day.

The heavy grinding sounds of the car hitting rumble strips on the side of the road caused my head to jerk up. *The guardrail is way too close! We're going to crash!*

This is going to be bad.

As the Pilot swerved, I immediately closed my eyes. *Lord, be with us! Show me how to pray!*

The car continued to swerve out of control. Then there was the sharp sound of glass shattering and heavier sounds of metal breaking.

Someone is screaming. I knew it was Andrea. My beautiful young daughter was screaming as if she were watching a horror movie unfold before her eyes.

Holy Spirit, show me how to pray!

I thought of the scripture that said, "My times are in your hands" (Psalm 31:15). *Maybe this is my time to die.*

Strangely, the realization that I might not live did not cause fear. Inside, I had a deep knowing that I would be in the presence of Christ if I were to die. I knew the Lord and I knew my soul would live on eternally with Him.

In those seconds of shattering, it was as if time stood still.

Thank you, Lord, for my life. Oh Lord, be with David and Champ. David, my eleven-year-old and Champ, my seven-year-old, were safe with their dad back in Montana.

Then the Holy Spirit dropped a thought in my mind. *Pray for a physician to arrive at the scene.*

That's an odd prayer. But I had asked the Holy Spirit how to pray. Who was I to question His leading?

The second prayer I prayed was for Andrea. *Lord Jesus, be close to Andrea.* I felt an urging, *Ask God to send someone to be with her.* My Mother's heart wanted her not to be alone. I wanted someone there who would take care of her, hug her, and reassure her that everything was going to be okay.

Lord, am I about to enter the gates of heaven and meet you? I knew in heaven I would be fine—I would be with the Lord and there would be no more sorrow, pain, or tears. But my prayers were now for my daughter. *Send someone to be her helper and friend!*

Shaken hard despite being strapped in my seat belt, I felt as if I was trapped in a metal container as the car careened from side to side. I braced myself for the coming crash and leaned back in my seat, pushing my right foot to the floorboard as if I was helping brake. I pressed myself into the floorboard of the car as if my life depended on it. As flying shards of glass exploded around me, I instinctively closed my eyes and mouth tightly.

The Pilot came to an abrupt and shuddering stop in a grassy area of median between north and southbound traffic on Highway 15.

I opened my eyes knowing I wasn't dead. *I'm still here. I can smell burning rubber. It must not be my time to die.*

Then the excruciating pain hit me. I knew I wasn't in heaven because there is no pain there.

A searing pain ripped through my body—the worst pain I had ever experienced in my forty-plus years of life. Not like childbirth when you know that in the end of all your contractions and hurt you will hold a beautiful baby. I wouldn't have wished this pain on my worst enemy.

Although I was in the grip of intense pain, I immediately turned to see how Andrea was. She was crying hysterically, but seemed to be uninjured.

Through her sobs, Andrea asked me, "Mom, are you OK?"

"It's just a car. The most important thing is we're both still alive." As her mother, I wanted to comfort and reassure.

We had both survived a very bad car accident. There was no fire. We had a lot to be grateful for. It didn't escape me that the car we had only nine days was beyond totaled.

It was then that I looked down and gasped. I was bleeding profusely. Chunks of flesh were missing from both of the backs of my lower calves. My right fibula, the bone from your knee to your ankle, was sticking straight up, and my right hip was in unbearable pain. My right hand had a cut on the top of it—and my ear was bleeding as well. It looked as if someone had thrown a grenade and aimed it at my legs and it had exploded in front of my face.

My whole body started to shake. *I'm going into shock. I can't pass out because I need to be here for Andrea. She needs her mom. What will happen to her without me?* I had to stay alert for her.

Then I saw movement outside as other travelers who had stopped to help gathered around what was left of the car. Just knowing they were there was comforting. We were not alone on the side of the freeway. I could hear their voices outside but they seemed to be coming through a tunnel far away.

"Has someone called 911?"

"How many are injured?"

"Can they get out of the car?"

In the chaos of noise around me, I heard a female voice saying, "Let me through. You really need to let me through! My name is Beth, and I am a physician."

At that very minute I felt the Lord's presence. His peace rushed over my body and into my spirit. *God, you are so good.*

Beth was the earthly physician that the Great Physician had sent in answer to prayer.

She began to evaluate me and then started asking for towels and blankets so she could tourniquet my legs. As my body shook from being in shock, she worked quickly on my legs to prevent me from losing even more blood. The blankets helped with the chills.

I never saw Dr. Beth's face; I just remember her voice and how competently she worked on me. I will probably never be able to thank her in person for her act of service and kindness. But I believe she played a major role in helping save my life. They told me later that I lost 75 percent of my blood at the scene of the accident. If it had not been for her care, I could have bled to death that night.

To me she was like an angel who swept down to do a job that God in His infinite care and concern had called her to specifically do that night. And then, poof! Dr. Beth was gone as if by the quick swish of a fairy wand after playing an important role to help save my life.

God had directly answered my prayers that night. I was left with a deep assurance that He was with me. This gave me the strength and confidence I needed. *Thank you for being with me, Lord. Help me through what is ahead!*

The wail of sirens in the distance broke into my thoughts. The ambulance arrived and the paramedics began to cut me out of the twisted vehicle. I looked up to see the face of a handsome paramedic who was working carefully and diligently to get me out of the car. It sounds like such a "girly" thing to say, but his handsome face helped me focus on something other than the excruciating pain I was feeling from all over my body. I saw it as a gift. *How good are you Lord to provide a handsome face as a distraction in the midst of all this mess of blood and brokenness?*

I was most conscious of the throbbing pain in my right hip. Something sharp seemed to have punctured it, and it was bleeding. My bones felt shattered.

I was so grateful to see Andrea was able to open her door and get out of the car. She only had a little cut on her arm but other than that she was spared injury. *Thank you Father for protecting my daughter and keeping her from injury.* As her mom, I was grateful I was the one going through this rather than her.

I was rushed to the closest trauma center, the Portneuf Medical Center in Pocatello, Idaho. In a burst of activity my jeans were cut off and tennis shoes removed. I could tell by the speed and focus of the ER doctors and nurses as they assessed my injuries that it was serious. Someone handed me a document to sign allowing a transfusion.

I was coherent enough to beg, "Please, don't cut my T-shirt." My Teanie Weanie Falls Brand team had won second place in the master's division for 2006, the previous year, and my souvenir Sawtooth Relay shirt was sacred to me. I had lost enough that night— I was not going to lose my hard-earned shirt too! The nurse got it off me without cutting it.

The Sawtooth Relay is a sixty-mile race I tried to do each year that starts in Stanley, Idaho and ends in Ketchum and travels through the breathtaking Sawtooth Mountains of Idaho and over Galena Pass. Now I wondered, *Will I ever race again?*

In all the chaos of the activity in the ER, I noticed a nurse who was talking to Andrea. Nurse Jenny was attentive, comforted her, and was watching out for her while the medical team was trying to stabilize me. The medical team was about to give me a pain shot and I knew I was about to enter "La-La Land." My daughter would be alone in the hospital—five hours from her dad and brothers in Montana and two-and-a-half hours from her friends, family friends, and any support system. At that moment, I remembered the second prayer I had prayed as we were crashing—that there would be someone there for Andrea so she would not be by herself. Watching Jenny with Andrea, I was comforted once again.

It was hard to concentrate on anything but the pain. On a scale of one to ten, my pain right then was about a twelve to fifteen! Part of me just wanted to surrender to the pain meds and not feel anything. I found myself having an interior dialogue with God. *Lord, it feels like heaven would have been the better choice right now.*

Again, I knew better than to question the Lord, the maker of heaven and earth, the creator and author of life, who was quite capable of ending my life at Milepost 95. He chose not to take my life, but to preserve it.

In the depths of incredible pain, I embraced the reality that God had answered my prayers. He had spared my life. While my body was in the midst of excruciating pain, my soul was at a deep level of peace. I was incredibly grateful. I remembered God's promise in His Word to watch over me wherever I go. *God, you never left me. You've been with me through it all.*

On July 1, 2007, the Lord of the universe answered two of what I thought were my last prayers on earth. I trusted Him to take care of me and my daughter and whatever would come next.

I had no way of knowing what some of those next things would be.

In Sickness and Health

I remain confident of this: I will see the goodness of the Lord in the
land of the living. Wait for the Lord; be strong and take heart and
wait for the Lord.

— Psalm 27:13–14

I WOKE UP IN a hospital room on oxygen at 10:00 a.m. the next day.
Andrea was sleeping peacefully in a chair beside my bed. *"Oh, thank you
Lord that Andrea is all right"* I breathed. I was deeply grateful she was
physically unscathed from the wreck.

When I looked down at myself, I looked like a character out of *The
Mummy.* Bandages were wrapped all over my body. I was hooked up to
a drip pump, but despite the morphine pumping through my body, I
was still in enormous pain. My lower extremities throbbed and ached.

"You're awake," commented a cheerful nurse entering my room.
She then began telling me about my injuries and how they were going
to care for me. Fuzzy from the pain meds, I struggled to comprehend
everything that had taken place.

Where is my husband? Matthew wasn't there, and this seemed odd to me. *Why is he not here?* The paramedic had called him from Andrea's cell phone in the ambulance the evening before. My cell phone had been lost in the wreck.

"Have you heard anything from my husband?" I asked a nurse. Matthew had taken a job in Montana, so he was five hours away by car.

"He's on his way."

A short time later, Carol Jones, a best friend, and her husband, Ron, arrived after driving an hour and a half from Twin Falls to Pocatello. While so glad to see Carol and Ron, who were such an encouragement and support, my thoughts kept going to my husband Matthew's absence. He was supposed to be my protector, provider, and lover and he wasn't by my side. *Where is he?*

Carol and Ron immediately saw what needed doing and started calling my parents, sister, and aunt in Virginia, giving them updates on how I was doing. It was hard for my parents not to be with me at this time of crisis but they were thousands of miles east, and two time zones ahead of us. Having Carol and Ron with me was evidence of the body of Christ at work in my hospital room, and their love made me feel loved and less alone.

The deep ache of my heart was palpable. I felt so alone and broken—just completely abandoned and alone. But into my mind dropped the comfort of Psalm 31:24: "Be strong and take heart, all you who hope in the Lord." I knew my hope had to be in the Lord and not just in my husband. *Thank you, Lord.* The word of God I had hidden in my heart began to settle my fears.

But I really wanted—no I needed—Matthew to be there by my side to comfort me. I couldn't understand his emotional disconnect. *Why isn't he able to be here for me?* He was a Christian therapist and counselor who should know all the right things to say or do. How could he be so unavailable like this?

I knew I had to press into Jesus as I had never done before. He was with me before the wreck, in the wreck, in the ER, and He was with me now. God had not abandoned or forsaken me. God was indeed my Immanuel—He was with me.

I tried to concentrate on what the doctor was saying. "You are going to need a couple of surgeries immediately." These were debridement surgeries to remove all the glass, metal, dirt, and debris from the open wounds on both of my legs. These had to be done prior to any other surgeries. Right then I was so exhausted that I just went along with whatever the medical staff told me would happen. I was broken and at their mercy to feel better; and I really wanted to start feeling better.

"Your right lower leg, the fibula, is broken and a rod will have to be inserted with screws. Your right pelvis is also shattered." The doctor added, "You are going to be non-weight-bearing for quite some time until your pelvis heals."

The pain in my broken pelvis made it too painful and almost impossible for me to move. Besides my broken right leg, I knew large portions of flesh had been torn out of my legs upon impact, because I had looked down on them after the accident.

I listened as the doctor went on and the news was not getting better. "You will require the use of wound vacs, vacuum-like machines with tubes hooked up to the portion of your body that has lost some flesh. The machines extract bacteria out of wounds and help prevent infection. Ultimately, they improve the circulation of the injured area and help speed up the healing process."

It was all so overwhelming. Surrendering to the pain medications, I drifted off to sleep.

Finally, thirty-six hours after the accident, Matthew walked into my hospital room. From his demeanor, he didn't seem to be upset at what had happened to me. He wasn't offering much sympathy or expressions of care after what we had gone through. I couldn't believe how completely unengaged he seemed. I had so hoped he would be present for me in every sense, but that didn't seem to be the case.

Matthew brought David and Champ to visit me. While it was so great to see my boys, I knew I had to look scary hooked up to tubes and machines in a hospital bed. Their mother who was normally in charge of taking care of them was lying helpless in bed and not able to do so. I hated that they had to see me all banged up. I wondered if their father had prepared them mentally and emotionally to see me in this condition.

Matthew arranged to stay several days with the boys in a house that Portneuf Medical Center rented out to families of patients in the hospital who did not live nearby, a Ronald McDonald type of home without the official title. Staying there would keep our family close during my hospitalization.

But, only a few days later, Matthew announced he was going back to Montana.

I began to panic. *What am I going to do? Who will take care of my boys, help Andrea get over the wreck, and help me recover?* I could do very little for myself and was told I'd be confined to a hospital bed for quite some time.

My mom and dad filled in the gap when they came out from Farmville, Virginia and stayed a week. They traveled back and forth from our house in Twin Falls to Pocatello two hours one way just to visit and care for me. Mom made necessary arrangements for my boys. Since my husband was making no plans to help out, my mom said she would be happy to stay and see me through my surgeries.

I spent the next twelve days at Portneuf Medical Center until I was stabilized and able to be transported to Magic Valley Regional Medical Center in Twin Falls, the hospital where I worked.

Prior to being transported to Twin Falls, the care team—all the nurses, doctors, therapists and discharge planners in charge of a patient's "care plan" —and my husband and parents got together to determine how I was going to be transferred from Pocatello to Twin Falls. The options were by ambulance, Lifeflight (a helicopter), or a friend's conversion van. Everyone carefully reviewed the possibilities and what insurance would cover.

Matthew, who had come back from Montana for a couple of days to check in on me, said, "You better not get to ride in a helicopter before I do." Normally, this would have been funny. It had always been a dream of his to ride in a helicopter. Despite my need for medical transportation, I knew he was dead serious and my heart dropped.

I looked over at my dad, who at this point looked livid, as if he could not believe what he had just heard. *How is it possible that my husband is making this all about him?*

It was decided that my friend Susie Peterson would transport me from Pocatello to Twin Falls in her conversion van. Mom would ride with us. I was so glad to be going to my hometown. I knew I would receive great care and encouragement from all the nurses and doctors I knew there. I realized I had a long road in front of me, but in Twin Falls I wouldn't feel as isolated as friends nearby could visit me more frequently.

That one-and-a-half-hour drive felt like an eternity. The conversion van was cozy and had very comfortable seating, and the nurses and my mom had added enough pillows to make it look like a Bed Bath and

Beyond display. But with my shattered pelvis I was still in quite a bit of pain. This was the first time I had been in a vehicle since the wreck, so I was nervous about being in traffic. With my vivid flashbacks from the accident, I felt traumatized about crashing again. The cars felt like they were traveling too fast or were too close. Susie was quite a trooper and an excellent chauffeur, but every bump or pebble on the freeway jostled me and my body ached. I chattered nonstop to keep my focus off my pain and anxiety.

When we finally arrived at Magic Valley Regional Medical Center, I felt so happy to be back in Twin Falls and pulling into the familiar parking lot. But it was humbling coming back as a patient. I was no longer the able-bodied and active coworker I had been in late June when I left for vacation from my job as the director of an injury prevention program for the hospital. A busy worker and mom with an active schedule, I was now returning to my hometown incapable of doing anything but lying on a bed. I wasn't happy that all the folks I knew and worked with were going to see me severely injured and not fully functioning. Externally, I was bandaged and frail looking. Inside, I was even more of an emotional basket case.

As we pulled up to the unloading area of the hospital I saw one of my dear friends, Jolene, a speech therapist at the hospital who had been a precious friend for several years. Our sons Champion and Ethan had met at preschool and over the years we had become good friends. I had watched her marriage dissolve and walked with her through her painful divorce. She had risen above the rubble and was both a wonderful mother and a successful professional.

When I saw Jolene, tears came to my eyes because she is the kind of friend who is like a ray of sunshine and a blessing all rolled into one. It felt as if God had sent her to be my welcoming committee. I was reminded of Proverbs 18:24: "One who has unreliable friends soon comes to ruin, but there is a friend who sticks closer than a brother."

At the curb, a couple of folks from transport had to try and figure out how to get me out of the van and carefully into the wheelchair and onto the sidewalk. Then the journey would continue down the sidewalk, into the hospital, through the corridors, and on the elevator to the TCU (Transitional Care Unit) of the hospital. Transport did an excellent job of getting me to the unit and it was great to be able to talk to Jolene along the journey. This was a distraction from all the folks looking at me along the way who were probably wondering what on earth had happened to me.

Nurses greeted me with smiles of encouragement. I was now in a room by myself that I would call "home" for the next thirteen days. Given the extent of my injuries and how vulnerable I felt, this was yet another blessing I received. A single room is one of the perks for hospital employees who become patients.

How can I be this exhausted when all I did was ride in a van? Along with my physical weakness, this had been an emotionally exhausting journey as well. After getting settled in my new bed, I ate something, swallowed a pain pill, and took a nap.

When I woke up, the director of the TCU, Janie Humphries came in to welcome me to her unit. Janie is one of the medical icons at our hospital and in our community. Standing by my bedside she let me know how sorry she was about the accident. "I want you to have a good experience on my unit and the best care possible." She then gave me her personal cell phone number and let me know that if I had any issues or problems that I could call her. I kept thinking, *Unbelievable! This is the royal treatment.* I felt very blessed and loved.

With lots of time to think, journal, and pray, Matthew's absence made my heart ache. I felt abandoned and alone. A year earlier he had left our family in Twin Falls to take a job in Montana. And while I'd been independent and caring for the children by myself during the year apart, now I keenly felt his absence. He wasn't with me during the most critical time in my life. My body was physically damaged, but the hurt and sadness I was feeling went far beyond what had happened to my body. The brokenness of my body reflected the chaos inside me.

How am I going to get through this? Must I literally be broken open to find the answer?

I had been thinking about the symbolism of broken shells ever since the mother of my best friend from high school, Monique, had sent me *My Beautiful Broken Shell: Words of Hope to Refresh the Soul* right after the accident. The words of hope in this book by Carol Hamblet Adams blessed and encouraged me to the depths of my soul.

> It is low tide and I watch, mesmerized, as the ocean rises slowly . . . curls . . . and then spills its white-laced foam onto the shore. I walk by a broken scallop shell . . . and leave it to search for more perfect ones. But then I stop . . . go back . . . and pick up the broken shell. I realize that this shell is me with my broken heart. This shell is people who are hurting . . . people who have lost loved ones . . . people who are frightened or alone . . . people with unfilled dreams. This shell has had to fight so hard to keep from totally being crushed by the pounding surf . . . just as I have had to. Yet this shell is still out on the beautiful sandy shore . . . just as I am. Thank you, Lord that I haven't been completely crushed by the heaviness in my heart . . . by the pounding of the surf.

I looked down at my bandaged body lying on the hospital bed and thought, *I am like a broken shell that is still beautiful in the eyes of the Lord.* I settled back on my pillow, still hurting, but taking comfort from that thought.

Deep Hunger

The shell must break before the bird can fly.

Alfred, Lord Tennyson

Then Jesus declared, "I am the bread of life. Whoever comes to me will never go hungry, and whoever believes in me will never be thirsty."

—John 6:35

THERE WAS INDEED A prior breaking of my shell, an initial breaking that led me to the end of myself and the beginning of my new life in Christ.

Let me tell you about myself. I was born into a good home with two loving parents. My sister Anne, who is four and a half years younger, and I were raised in a home with no abuse, no addictions. Our home was a good and safe place to grow up.

My dad, Marvin, has a PhD in botany and was a professor at Longwood College (now Longwood University where the Democratic debates were held in 2016) in my hometown of Farmville, Virginia.

My mom, Lee Warriner Scott, was a student at Longwood when they started dating, and they have now been married almost fifty-six years.

I was the firstborn and the first grandchild on each side of my family. According to Dr. Kevin Leman in *The Birth Order Book,* the qualities of a firstborn are: "perfectionistic, reliable, conscientious, a list maker, well organized, hard driving, a natural leader, critical, serious, scholarly, logical, and one who doesn't like surprises." That's me!

Our home was a very moral and Christian home. We were expected to use good manners, be polite, follow directions, keep a neat room, do chores, and always do our best. If my mom worked outside the home it was only part-time, so she was there to take my sister and me to dance, debate practice, piano lessons, softball, or other activities.

Growing up in a southern town of about five thousand people in the Commonwealth of Virginia, there were other rules that were important. You could only wear white shoes after Memorial Day and never after Labor Day. "Yes ma'am" and "No ma'am" were important words used every day. We were always expected to be home for the family dinner hour. My mom is a great cook and we always had fresh vegetables from the garden and homemade casseroles. My dad is an avid hunter so usually the meal had some rendition of deer meat or wild turkey or whatever creature my dad had hunted, gathered, and put in the freezer.

Regular church attendance was a part of the southern culture and was expected by everyone.

My parents were and still are members of the Farmville Presbyterian Church. My sister and I were baptized there as infants and grew up going to Sunday school and catechism class where we memorized the Apostle's Creed. We attended vacation Bible school and summer camp each year.

I was a Brownie, and a Girl Scout, and a lead cookie seller in my troop, which is in line with the "hard driving" firstborn characteristics. I'd make my lists of all the folks who I would approach about selling cookies and then would call them up on our rotary telephone.

In high school, I played softball on a summer league, however, I really was not a good player at all; this was not my forte. I went through the motions of playing the game, but I'd be in the outfield thinking of all the other things I could be doing such as gathering daisies or dandelions and making dandelion chains.

My elementary school experience at the John P. Wynne Campus School from kindergarten through seventh grade was wonderful. This was one of those "lab" schools where many student teachers from Longwood College did their student teaching. With observation windows everywhere, many days we felt like guinea pigs being observed in a laboratory with special notes being written down about us as students.

Once seventh grade ended we had two choices for high school: Prince Edward Academy—a completely all-white school or—Prince Edward County High School, which was about 90 percent African American.

This was 1978 in the South, and there were still some pretty significant racial lines that had been drawn in the sand in Farmville.

My dad was on the school board for Prince Edward County High School, the public school in my town, but my parents left the choice of which school I wanted to attend up to me. I stood in front of the mirror in my lemon chiffon bedroom trying to make this decision. I had been raised in the church, but as a seventh grader did not have a personal relationship with Christ. I vividly remember thinking, *God created both whites and blacks.* I felt very strongly that He also probably meant for us to be in school *together and not separated or segregated.*

Coming out of my room, I marched down our hallway to proclaim to my parents, "I've made my choice. I'm going to go to Prince Edward County High School." This seemed like a logical choice to me.

As I entered high school in 1979, I longed to be successful academically and to be accepted socially as well. I had been the freckly faced girl who got glasses in third grade and I had never quite felt like I fit in or belonged anywhere.

I joined the debate team so I could use my serious, aggressive, and conscientious traits. Mom thought I got my excellent debate skills from arguing with our family at home. Our debate team was a close-knit group of determined and academic students, among them: Amanda McCombs, Clifford Peale (the grandson of the late Norman Vincent Peale), Sandra Kiess, and my debate partner, Monique Renee Fawcett. Our debate coach Nancy Phaup was much more than a coach; she was a mentor, cheerleader, and a second mom to all of us on the team. She went above and beyond the call of duty to ensure that we had excellent debate experiences. Several years in a row we won state titles.

My social life in high school was not the greatest—studying and preparing for debate tournaments was about the extent of it. I had to keep up with homework during the week because just about every weekend of the debate season we would travel almost the whole weekend to a tournament or competition.

I desperately wanted to be loved and accepted and to feel good about myself. I was a medium build, not overweight, but my mom would often describe me as having "broad shoulders."

In contrast, my sister, Anne, had a very petite frame and was tall and thin. She was also academically strong, a dancer, coordinated, and very popular in school—unlike me. She seemed to always have a boyfriend and a date for a dance or a prom—sometimes even multiple invitations for a date! I compared myself to her quite a lot. We were close growing up and are still very close; she is precious to me. I don't think she knew how often I compared myself with her while we were growing up. But the truth was, I was just struggling with my own self-image like many teenagers do. It was absolutely nothing that she did, just my own issues and insecurities.

My life started to unravel somewhere between my junior and senior year in high school. I was heading to college and so badly wanted to be thin and popular and asked out on dates. *Maybe I will bloom and flourish when I get to college*, I hoped.

To help things along, I started dieting and exercising like a fiend. Monique, who had been my best friend since we met in preschool/kindergarten, and I had gotten jobs as lifeguards at Longwood College. After lifeguarding we'd either go in early and swim a mile or stay late after we worked and swim a mile. We also started bike riding and had a twelve-mile route that we would do on the back roads.

I started taking college classes during the summers in high school to get ahead. I took weight lifting and training and I loved it. This was my first exposure to a class where I could build muscle and make my body more toned and in shape. I loved how this made me feel, how I was starting to look, and the extra energy that weight lifting was giving me. People began commenting on my new tone and shape and thinner body and I sure liked the attention.

I began skipping meals, did not eat much at all at mealtimes when I did eat, and drank a ton of Diet Coke so my stomach felt full. I did not realize I was at the beginning of what would lead to an eating disorder. My tendency to please people and have a perfect body was starting to take over with a vengeance. I was headed down a path of destruction with no idea how it would affect me.

"Why don't you want some of this?" Mom would ask, obviously exasperated because whatever she made, I wouldn't eat. She tried to make things lean and without fat or butter but I wouldn't even try it.

My senior year I weighed 103 pounds at 5' 6" and was a size three! It was a glorious time for me. To top it off, I was voted the senior class "Best Dieter" award. What more could a girl ask for?

My parents were beside themselves. No matter what they said or tried to do, I did not change my behavior. I became secretive about what I ate, when I ate, and how much I exercised. My rule was if I ate something, I had to do an activity to burn all the calories off.

In the early eighties there was not a lot of information and research on eating disorders but it was starting to be recognized and noticed. As teenage girls, we compared ourselves to super-thin models and actresses. Parents didn't find it socially acceptable then to talk to their friends or anyone else about concerns they might have about their child's eating habits.

My parents worried about my health and took me to doctors and tried to coax me to eat. However, like many anorexics, I was determined and stubborn. I wanted to be thin, and no talking or trying to coerce me worked. They were probably hoping that my change of scene in college would help.

I graduated from high school in June of 1983 and that fall went off to Virginia Tech where I majored in communication studies, specifically public relations as I wanted to work with the public.

That first year was a rough one with all the adjustments of college, a roommate, classes, and finals. My roommate and I were not that compatible so there was friction there and I wasn't comfortable in the one room I could call my own on campus. My cubicle in the Newman Library became my second home. I could study without being interrupted there and no one bothered me.

The inevitable occurred as I threw myself even more into academic success, exercising, and dieting. My daily intake of food was normally a can of tuna, some green peas and a lot of Diet Coke. I tried to not eat more than three hundred calories for the whole day. Some days I would drink an entire six-pack of Diet Coke to make myself feel full.

Eating so few calories and exercising like a maniac, coupled with studying five to ten hours a day on top of going to classes made for a pretty rigorous schedule. No wonder I felt lousy most of the time. My body obviously needed more nutrients, but I was determined to do whatever I needed to do to stay at my ideal weight of 105. I made all sorts of vows and promises to myself so I wouldn't go above that weight.

But my life was about to change through those who God was bringing into my life.

Satisfied

The Lord has established his throne in the heaven, and his kingdom rules over all.

—Psalm 103:19

GOD HAD PLACED ME right where He wanted me—wouldn't you know—in a dorm full of Christian women. Everywhere I turned I seemed to run into a woman full of a foreign-to-me type of peace and assurance. *What is it about these women?* I wondered.

One night as I was leaving the library from a full day and night of studying, I walked out the door at the same time as another coed. We seemed to always walk out at the same time—usually closing time. Marsha Brown and I started a conversation and I found out she lived in my dorm. That night was the beginning of an amazing friendship that is still intact twenty-plus years later.

I started hanging out with Marsha and the other women she was friends with in our dorm. They belonged to a group called InterVarsity Christian Fellowship—a group of Christians who met for worship, Bible studies, and discipleship on campus.

These students were unlike any others I had ever met. They were serious about their commitment and their relationship with God and with each other. They were nice, respectful, and didn't drink or smoke. While full of peace, they also had fun and laughed a lot. These women would often go with me to get something to eat, even though they had already eaten. They were concerned about me and would do these gestures of love for my sake.

At this point, because of my eating disorder and lack of body fat, my menstrual cycle had been absent almost three years. A doctor I went to warned me saying, "If you do not start taking care of yourself, eating better, and gaining weight, you might not be able to have children down the road." Being fertile and conceiving a child wasn't relevant to me then, so I was not too worried about this. My goal was to be thin, look good, and be accepted.

Back at home after my freshman year I continued my anorexic behavior and worked to keep my weight low.

When I did not make the lottery for a dorm room for my sophomore year, I needed to find an apartment to live in. I saw an advertisement on a bulletin board for someone who needed a roommate. Margie was a serious student, had great morals, and seemed like a great gal, and I felt like we hit it off. I signed a lease to join her in the Sturbridge Square Apartments.

Our first two quarters were a bit rocky. I was very moody because I did not eat enough or sleep enough—all I did was study and exercise. I didn't keep much food in the apartment so it would not be a temptation. Then I'd just be absolutely starving and would sneak some of Margie's food and eat it. I was not able to purge and throw up any food that I had eaten. If I felt I had eaten too much, I just exercised more or took laxatives to get rid of the calories.

Obviously, this created tension between us as roommates. Margie wanted to help me get better but did not know how. I just wanted her to stay out of my business and let me be thin and work out.

"Page, please come with me to my church tomorrow," Margie asked me one Saturday night.

"Sorry, Margie, I can't. I have to study and exercise."

That night alone in my bedroom, I felt as if there was an intense struggle going on inside my soul. I felt the closest I had ever felt to committing suicide. *I don't want to live anymore. Life is too hard.* It was as if I was wrestling with God and He and the devil were fighting for my soul.

The pressure I put myself under for grades and maintaining a size three was too much. That quarter I had made the dean's list—one of my personal goals. I desperately wanted my parents' approval but felt as if I would never achieve that. I felt as if I was always falling short in some capacity. My parents, of course, wanted me to make good grades and be successful academically, but I was the one putting most of the pressure on myself. I wanted to make perfect grades. I felt empty, worthless, and had no peace or contentment.

I came out of my bedroom and in desperation said, "Margie? Can we talk?"

For the first time, I opened up to Margie and began to share my pain.

"What can I do to help?" Margie asked. "Can I have my friend Wendy come over?" She was probably looking for moral support in knowing how to deal with me.

"Yeah, you can invite your friend Wendy over. And tell her to bring her *sword* and her *shield*." I have no idea why I used those words. I didn't know it then, but Wendy had been instrumental in leading Margie to the Lord a couple weeks prior to that night. Wendy came over and we three talked for a long time.

I woke up Sunday morning determined not to give in and go with Margie to church. *How will that help anyway?* I stumbled through the dining room as I made my way to the kitchen for a Diet Coke. I spotted a note for me on the dining room table with Margie's Bible open to a passage of scripture. Her note said, "I thought this scripture might minister to you and encourage you." I sat down and read Ephesians 6:12–17 in Margie's Bible for the first time.

> For our struggle is not against flesh and blood, but against the rulers, against the authorities, against the powers of this dark world and against the spiritual forces of evil in the heavenly realms. Therefore put on the full armor of God, so that when the day of evil comes, you may be able to stand your ground, and after you have done everything, to stand. Stand firm then, with the belt of truth buckled around your waist, with the breastplate of righteousness in place, and with your feet fitted with the readiness that comes from the gospel of peace. In addition to all this, take up the shield of faith, with which you can extinguish all the flaming arrows of the evil one. Take the helmet of salvation and the sword of the Spirit, which is the word of God.

As I read these verses I felt a deep sense of awe. *How does Margie know what is going on in my mind and heart?* For the first time in my life I experienced a sense of the power of the Holy Spirit. Despite our conversation the night before, there was no way that Margie could have known about the battle going on inside of me.

I immediately went to my room to dress for church. I was not about to argue with the power of the Holy Spirit.

That Sunday I went to church with Margie, Wendy, and her fiancé, Rob.

God has an incredible sense of humor. Margie had wanted me to go to her church that Sunday because a certain pastor was to preach that day. But when we got there, he wasn't there. The assistant pastor gave the message that day.

I learned it doesn't have to be a specific person to lead a person to Christ. When God wants you to hear the message of the gospel He uses whomever He pleases to accomplish this task.

That morning the associate pastor talked about believing in Christ and then having a relationship with Christ by accepting Him as Savior. I listened intently as he shared Acts 16:31: "Believe in the Lord Jesus, and you will be saved—you and your household."

I sat there thinking, *Wow, is that all I have to do to have the peace that my friends have? Seriously—is that all I have to do?*

There was an altar call when people were invited to the front to pray. I looked over at Margie and Wendy. Margie looked at me and said, "You need to do this for yourself, not for me or for Wendy. If you go down front it is because you want this relationship with Christ for yourself."

On that Palm Sunday in 1985 I walked down the aisle and accepted Christ as my Lord and Savior. I walked out of that Pentecostal church filled with a freedom and a peace I had never before known. I felt different and even the sky seemed bluer and the sun brighter.

Looking back on that day, I truly believe the Lord had to save me spiritually so He could then start healing my physical body from the eating disorder. My spiritual house had to be restored before the physical restoration could begin.

I did not go home that day and order Domino's pizza and bake brownies and eat them. Healing is often a process. In my case, it was a gradual process of going to counseling, learning how to eat, not being afraid that if I ate a meal I would gain five pounds or go up a size in pants.

Had God not placed the InterVarsity people, and Margie and Wendy in my life at that time I firmly believe I would not have lived much longer. Anorexia would have killed me. The disease would have won and not the Lord and the Holy Spirit.

I got a ride home the next weekend to surprise my parents and let them know that I had accepted Christ as my Lord and Savior. I wanted to hopefully allay any fears they had about me doing further damage to myself with the eating disorder.

After I had shared with my parents about my conversion, Dad and Uncle Ken, my dad's only brother, came into my room with me and told me they had prayed for my salvation and healing. My uncle, a physician, knew of the physical damage I had done to myself because of the eating disorder and was in tears as he shared this with me. I attribute my salvation to his prayers and the prayers of other faithful saints and intercessors who carried me to the throne of grace.

In reading the Bible, I learned from 1 Corinthians 3:16 that my body was the temple of God and His Spirit was now living in me. Once I realized this, I started thinking about what I needed to eat and how to better take care of myself. Jesus had not only saved my soul, but He was saving me from living with a horrible disease. Gradually, I gained a desire to eat better. My fear of food lessened. I realized food was not the enemy; God had created food to nourish and strengthen our bodies.

My coming to faith in God, and His healing of my eating disorder, and the protection and care He had on my body years before the accident, was a demonstration of His faithfulness that has carried me through all the years.

As I learned about God's goodness, and faithfulness, and His new mercies every day, I gained both the internal and external strength to trust Him. I was learning God is always with me; He never leaves me. I knew beyond a shadow of a doubt that He would always be there for me, whatever the circumstance.

For years, I had been trying to be accepted and loved by others—peers, men, parents, and family members. The empty hole that had been so deep in my body was really a God-sized hole that I was trying to fill with everything *but* God—being thin, academics, high grades, the dean's list, and staying a size three. My deep personal hunger was not for those fleeting things. That deep hunger was only satisfied by the love of the Lord and the joy His salvation brought me.

I joined InterVarsity Christian Fellowship on campus and became a student leader—a large group coordinator—with the organization. During the next two and a half years, I grew tremendously in my faith as I was discipled by a wonderful Christian woman, Susan Anderson (Wampler).

When I had the eating disorder, I always wrestled with my self-image. As my healing gradually took place, I learned to take those thoughts to the cross and not allow the devil to have a foothold in that area at all. I found that true healing from an eating disorder comes from knowing my identity in Christ and seeing myself as He sees me. I was so grateful to the Lord for making all things new in my life. He has been the healer of both my heart and my body. Understanding God's love and acceptance of me was a huge milepost in my healing.

The rest of my college years were incredibly excellent. But I longed for a man to love and have companionship with. Knowing the damage that I had done to my body, I prayed that I would eventually meet a strong Christian man and be able to have a family one day.

The One

Two are better than one, because they have a good return for their labor.

—Ecclesiastes 4:9

MATTHEW AND I MET at a prayer conference at Wheaton College when I was twenty-seven years old and he was thirty-one. I was attracted to him because on the outside he seemed worshipful as well as intelligent. At the prayer conference, I had admired him from afar and thought, *This guy seems like a great guy and a wonderful Christian man.* He seemed to love to worship and was committed to prayer and that appealed to me.

The first night we met we talked on bleachers outside of a dorm at the college until the wee hours of the morning. We discovered in our conversation that we had a lot of family values and beliefs in common.

Both our fathers had pursued careers in science—my dad as a professor in botany and biology, and his dad as a brilliant chemist and professor. Despite his father's intellect and successful career, his father struggled with mental illness and had taken his own life when Matthew was only five years old. Both our mothers had master's degrees in English.

As we continued to talk that humid night in Illinois, I learned that Matthew had been married before. The relationship had been short-lived and ended in divorce. He had a daughter from that marriage who was three years old. His first wife had abandoned both their marriage and motherhood when their daughter was only fifteen months old.

When we finally stopped talking, we realized how late it was. We were locked out of the dorm and had to tap loudly on the glass to have a security guard let us into our respective dorm rooms. As we said goodnight, I wondered, *What will happen next?*

Just then Matthew asked, "Do you want to have breakfast with me in the morning?"

I didn't sleep much that night. I felt excited and nervous thinking about my conversation with this handsome and intelligent man who loved the Lord.

The rest of the conference we spent our free time talking and sharing about our walks with the Lord. When the conference came to an end, I wondered, *what will happen to our connection? Will I ever see this man again? Has this been just a "chance" meeting that will go nowhere?* After all, we lived far apart. Matthew lived in Eugene, Oregon and I lived in Lexington, Kentucky.

The last day of the conference Matthew asked, "Can I write you and call you to see where things might lead?"

I happily said yes. But still I wondered, *Is Matthew "the one" God has for me?*

I had dated very little in college, focusing on doing well academically, graduating, and deepening my relationship with the Lord and my friendships. I had started a career in public relations, been involved in some great churches and singles' groups. But I had never met anyone whom I felt I could be "in love" with.

Truth be told, I was looking for love and wanting to get married. Most of my friends were already married or in serious relationships. Part of me felt a bit desperate. *If I don't get married soon, it might not ever happen!*

After the conference our long-distance relationship began. His letters started to come in the mail and we often talked on the phone. Most of our courtship was via letters in the mail and phone visits. We were three time zones apart so we talked late at night for hours when we had both finished our busy days.

I had pretty high expectations for a man—a man of faith, prayerful, and spiritually sound. Also, I wanted someone who liked the outdoors, hiking, and physical activities as much as I did. I longed to have a companion to do activities with.

Matthew asked me to come visit him in Eugene. I was excited but also nervous about meeting three-year-old Andrea. She turned out to be a beautiful and smart little redhead with a wonderful personality. I had dreamed of adopting a little redheaded girl since I was about thirteen, so this felt like one of the missing puzzle pieces of God's perfect plan.

At first, she was not sure what to think of me, but after a while she warmed up to me. I had brought her a few presents that I thought three-year-old girls would like so that was a winning factor. After several encounters, she seemed to realize I was not taking her dad away; she was gaining another person in her life.

Matthew and I saw each other about once a month. We had some fun visits hanging out, hiking, and spending time together. We incorporated the Lord into our relationship by going to church together and doing things with the folks whom I worked with in ministry.

Then came the weekend that I knew Matthew was going to propose. That was not our greatest visit or date. We fought a lot that weekend.

When it was time for dinner we fought about where to go for the date. I wanted to go to a more formal place but he did not.

At the end of the meal at the Merrick, a restaurant in Lexington I excused myself to go to the restroom. As I walked away from the table, I thought, *This has not been a storybook evening for sure. He probably won't even propose tonight.*

But when I returned to my seat Matthew pulled out a little ring box and got down on one knee and asked, "Will you marry me?"

I looked down at the beautiful gold band with an emerald on each side of a center diamond and oohed and aahed at the ring. I had mentioned to him that I loved emeralds because the green reminds me of growing together with him in the Lord. And the center diamond signified Christ as the center of our relationship.

I looked into his eyes and quickly said, "Yes!"

This must be God's will and best for me. I felt time was ticking away—I needed to marry this godly man, adopt his daughter, and let the life I had always dreamed of begin.

We set our wedding date for June 11, 1994—almost a year to the date of our initial meeting at Wheaton College. We had only spent about five times together prior to getting engaged—and all of that courtship had been in a long-distance relationship.

There was a minor matter: Matthew was not gainfully employed when we met. He was volunteering for a Christian ministry in Eugene and he and Andrea were living in a trailer. I should have done more research on his employment background. This was a guy with a master's degree but no paying job.

Later on in our marriage, steady employment and keeping jobs turned out to be a pattern, and not a good one. He would often become discontent and want to pursue something else. His work history during our married life was not the most stable.

But I was stepping out in faith and trusting God, right? I had a full-time job, so together we decided that he and Andrea would move to Kentucky where my job was and we would live there.

In the late winter of 1993, I flew to Colorado and helped Matthew and Andrea move across the country. This was a fairly good adventure as Andrea was a fantastic traveler and we did not have inclement winter weather.

Matthew and Andrea moved into a two-bedroom townhouse that I would eventually move into once we were married.

During this time, I had what I considered my dream job as a campus pastor with InterVarsity Christian Fellowship at the University of Kentucky. I enjoyed helping students come to Christ, grow in their relationship with Him through discipleship, teaching the word of God, and helping students pursue their call to missions, ministry, or servanthood in the marketplace.

I had moved from Madison, Wisconsin in 1992 where I had worked in public relations and marketing for 2100 Productions, the media arm of InterVarsity's ministry. Working at their corporate headquarters was an amazing experience. I worked with and was discipled by many wonderful women and men of God whom I am still friends with. I worked on an Urbana Missions Conference—the largest conference in the world that calls students to missions abroad.

In 1991, I had the incredible opportunity of traveling to Russia on a Lingua cultural exchange where we took nineteen students from all over the United States on a six-week mission trip. This was my first mission trip and it forever changed me and grew my heart for missions. I came back with a deeper desire to do more missions projects and to be a part of God's work in other countries.

However, the harsh winters in Wisconsin took a toll on me so I transferred to Kentucky—back to the South! You can take the girl out of the South, but not the South out of the girl. I am a true G. R. I. T.—girl raised in the South.

As the only single female on our ministry team at the University of Kentucky, each day I had the privilege of having Bible studies, prayer, and discipleship with women on the campus. Since I had come to Christ largely through this ministry at Virginia Tech, I wanted to be able to give back a little of what God had given me. Just as I had been an unsaved, struggling college student stumbling to find peace and truth, I now met with similar students and could understand where they were coming from. Better yet, I could share my testimony of coming to Christ and being led to peace, grace, mercy, and forgiveness. And most importantly, gaining eternal life, and learning to live life abundantly with Christ.

I had a desire to help start an international ministry there. With the blessing of my boss, I ministered to many Malaysian students and other nationalities attending UK as well. I heard stories of students being rejected by their family and friends when they made decisions to follow the Lord. Fathers beat daughters when they turned away from Buddha and made Jesus their Lord and Savior. Sons and daughters were disowned by their families because of their allegiance to Christ and His word.

I was so privileged to work under and with some phenomenal Christian leaders who are still near and dear to my heart. Mack and Leanne Stiles, Brian and Joanne Parks, David and Kris Lawrence, and David and Angie McNeill made a huge impact on my life and were incredible examples of godly marriages and walking out their faith in their families. The way they loved each other and their children continues to minister to me in tremendous ways.

I think in many ways I wanted what these leaders had, and thought by marrying Matthew this would all magically happen. When some of the people I worked with expressed concerns about me marrying him, I didn't heed their counsel and let my heart jump ahead of my mind.

My wedding planning began. Every girl's dream of a lifetime, right? As we started planning we seemed to disagree a lot and butt heads on things. Matthew was a mountaineer who liked things simple, and a northern guy from upstate New York.

As a southern girl, I wanted the traditional wedding with flowers, cake, and tons of family and friends present. I was a "detail-diva bride" holding out for southern charm and elegance!

Matthew was not very into the wedding planning and not much help at all. In fact, we were not partners from the get-go in many areas. This should have been another sign to me of our incompatibility, but I let my heart once again get ahead of the practicalities of our relationship.

We did manage to agree on getting married at the Asbury Theological Seminary in Wilmore, Kentucky. So on a beautiful warm Saturday in June, Matthew and I were united in marriage surrounded by dear family and friends. My sister, Anne Scott Meehan, and friend Marsha Brown Jordan were my maids of honor and Rachel Hasty Matthews was my bridesmaid.

Rachel made a beautiful wedding cake, an elaborate piece of art and confection that she transported all the way from North Carolina to Kentucky. Three hearts on top were joined together by ribbon signifying the joining of not only a husband and wife, but a family as well. The icing was an elaborate strawberry buttercream—Rachel's special recipe.

It was so hot in the reception hall the day of the wedding that Rachel had to turn the fans on to keep the icing from melting.

Our weeklong honeymoon was on Dog Island, a barrier island off Florida, donated to us by Wayne and Beth Williams, the pastor of the church we attended in Lexington.

Things were looking up. Right before we were married, Matthew's master's degree in human resources landed him a job at the Toyota plant right outside of Kentucky. I felt reassured as we started our married life together with two incomes.

I knew going into the marriage that it was a package deal. I had not planned to be a new wife and a mom at the same time, but God gave me the grace and energy to do so. The daily addition of a child to the mix was an adjustment as my routine now included picking Andrea up from daycare and her preschool activities.

After we had another week of adjusting to being a couple at home, I started potty training Andrea at night. She was awesome and it only took a couple of days.

Andrea was an easy preschooler and made the transition into our new family unit easily. She was very creative and loved to look at books, build things, and learned to read at a young age. She would play quietly in her room with her Bryer horses and Calico Critters. She was a great first child and I never considered her a burden, only a blessing.

I did not want to be a stepmom; I wanted to adopt Andrea. Once we were officially engaged, I called up Andrea's biological mom and asked if she would be willing to give up her parental rights and allow me to adopt Andrea. We chatted for about forty-five minutes and she asked me some questions and then agreed to start the legal paperwork. She was living in another state so it took about a year for the interstate adoption to become final.

In March of 1995, the year after we got married, I officially adopted Andrea and obtained parental rights from her biological mother who had been absent in her life since she was fifteen months old.

My relationship with Matthew continued to grow as we shared day-to-day things in life together—meals, long walks, and other outside activities. We found a church, the Lexington Evangelical Free church, and pursued joining this church together. This was a fun time of life as we developed some relationships with other young couples and families. We would enjoy spontaneous get-togethers and picnics and celebrate our children's birthdays together. It was an incredibly enjoyable stage of life and a wonderful place to live.

That fall of 1995, unexpectedly, we found out our lives were about to change in a big way.

Growing Pains

Swim through your troubles. Run to the promises, they are our Lord's branches hanging over the water so that His children may take a grip of them.

—Samuel Rutherford

WHEN WE FOUND OUT we were expecting our first child together, I felt excited and scared at the same time. The doctors had told me in college that I might not be able to conceive, so we were not really "trying" or "trying not to," but there I was, pregnant.

How will I handle two kids and a full-time job? We made the decision that I would go part-time to take some of the pressure off me at home and at work. It reassured me to know that Matthew had a full-time job while I helped support our family.

On June 28, 1996, David Scott Geske was born into our family—our first son. I had prepared for the birth experience naturally with the Bradley Method of childbirth. We had created a birth plan that included no drugs whatsoever as I wanted a completely natural, drug-free birth.

I felt I was in good hands with our wonderful Christian gynecologist, Dr. David Hagar.

I felt God created us to have children so I shouldn't need drugs or epidurals to do this. After all, women all over the world squat to give birth, and have normal and healthy babies.

I worked out at the gym and fast walked up until delivery day. I was careful what I ate and drank and gave up caffeine and wine the moment I found out I was expecting.

My actual due date was June 24, but that day our son did not enter this world. I did, however, end up in the hospital.

I was on my way to pick up Andrea from Bible school and was involved in a fender bender. Because I was nine months pregnant and my stomach had hit the steering wheel, they took me to the hospital and hooked me up to a fetal monitor to make sure that the baby was okay, and that there was no internal bleeding or puncturing of the placenta.

I saw the goodness of God in those four hours of hospitalization as it prepared me for my delivery and calmed my nerves about delivering. I met all the staff that day and knew I would be in capable hands once the big day arrived.

Three days later I went into labor. When the nurses took my vitals, my blood pressure was much higher than it was supposed to be and it was determined I had labor-induced toxemia. The nurses told me I needed to be hooked up to an IV with magnesium sulfate, a drug that reduces blood pressure as well as prevents grand mal seizures.

"This will slow down your labor process," a nurse told me. I would have to be lying down and on my side during labor. If you know anything about preparing for natural childbirth, this is the antithesis of the position you want to be in.

I was not a happy camper. I had prepared for nine months to have this baby naturally and now, completely out of my control, I had to work extra hard to do so.

Doctor Hagar informed me, "If you can't push the baby out yourself, a C-section may be necessary."

I thought, *I am going to use every ounce of strength in me to have this baby on my own.*

My good friend Carolyn Sizemore arrived on the scene to help with birth coaching. She had been my inspiration for natural childbirth when a year prior to this, I had been in the labor room with her and watched her deliver her youngest son, Isaac, naturally. She was my natural-birth guru so I was happy to have her with me.

"You can do this, Page. Just listen to your body and work with it," Carolyn said.

Matthew was in the room as well but wasn't very engaged or present. When I first went into labor at home, he had walked down the block with me, then announced, "I need to go take a nap so I'll be awake for the labor."

During labor at the hospital, he seemed to be preoccupied. He left to get something to eat a couple of times when I was in intense labor. This was not the behavior that I had envisioned with the birth of our first child together and my first delivery. Honestly, I was hoping for more partnership and encouragement.

Finally, Carolyn had to leave because she needed to get home to take care of Isaac and her other two children.

The labor continued for hours and hours, and I was worn out and exhausted.

"Do babies ever get stuck, and don't come out?" I asked the nurse.

She chuckled and said, "Oh, they come out all right, just in their own time, not ours."

Between contractions I prayed, "Father, please help this baby to come out. You know how much I do not want to have a C-section."

Within moments it was as if God knew my body was depleted. Our David came into this world naturally, without a C-section, or pain meds of any kind, after twenty-one hours of labor with toxemia and magnesium sulfate—against all odds!

He was a beautiful and healthy baby boy. Despite being unavailable during the birthing process, Matthew seemed thrilled to have a son. We named him David, to honor Matthew's deceased father, and Scott as a middle name, my maiden name to honor my father. David Scott means "beloved strong one"—quite a fitting name from the beginning of his life until now. He is my beloved firstborn son and is an amazingly strong and physical soccer player. It is his passion and drive for life!

Five days after David's delivery I began having intense headaches and I didn't feel good at all. On the Friday after the weekend when David was born, I felt so bad I drove myself to the emergency room to be checked out. The post-partum nurses took my blood pressure and said it was a bit elevated, but not high enough to warrant concern. They gave me pain medicine and advised me to go home and try to sleep. If I didn't feel any better in the morning, or if I got worse, then I was to come back.

The next day I woke up feeling much worse and again drove myself to the hospital, leaving baby David with Matthew. This time my blood pressure was high above what it was supposed to be.

"You have postpartum induced toxemia," the nurse said. I would need to be admitted and put on magnesium sulfate for at least twenty-four hours to try to bring down my blood pressure.

I burst into tears on hearing this. Then I called Matthew to let him know I was being admitted and that he would need to bring David to "room in" with me. Since David was being breastfed I could have him in the hospital with me while they got my blood pressure under control.

I was admitted, and the IV flowing with magnesium sulfate started pumping through my body. This is truly a drug from hell. It made me feel hot and bad and it burned as it went into my veins and body.

When Matthew brought David to me, my son was completely resilient and fine. His mother, on the other hand, was not the happiest mother on the block. My parents were to arrive at our house any time to meet their first biological grandson. I wanted to show them our new son in the comfort of our rented duplex, and not a hospital room. Matthew taped a note on our door directing my parents to Central Baptist Hospital and that's where my parents met David.

With our newly expanded family, we hoped to purchase our first home. We found a beautiful, three-bedroom house with an office, den, and living room that seemed the perfect fit for us. It was on a lovely cul-de-sac in an older neighborhood of Lexington, within walking distance from some of our best friends from church. My parents graciously gave us some money to help with the down payment so we could purchase the home. It was a wonderful feeling to finally have a place of our own.

However, less than a year later, Matthew got restless in his job at Toyota and wanted to pursue something else. His paternal grandfather, August Geske, had recently passed away and left him some money. Matthew decided to use that money to pursue graduate school and a master's degree in counseling. He found a school in Seattle, Washington that suited his desires and theology regarding Christian counseling, Mars Hill Graduate School, now the Seattle School of Theology and Psychology. This would be his second graduate degree.

Thinking about moving was hard for me. I had come to love the staff at InterVarsity, and their examples of godliness were incomparable to anything I had ever experienced before. I dearly loved my students and hated to have to say good-bye to them.

I loved our first house and neighborhood—it seemed storybook-perfect to me. We had a great church, support system, and incredible fellowship with some of the best friends in the world. There was a sense of community there that I have never experienced since. We would watch each other's kids, and share meals and all our joys and sorrows.

Nina Kinnicutt was a nurse who stayed home with her son Jonathan, and she had been the in-home daycare provider for David while I worked part-time. It was an excellent arrangement for childcare. A godly and loving woman was taking care of David for me so I could do my ministry work.

We put our house up for sale and it sold in record time. After downsizing, we packed up for the move to a two-bedroom townhouse we were purchasing in Bothell, Washington, close to the seminary.

Andrea was seven and David almost two when we moved across the country to Bothell. We celebrated David's second birthday in Columbia, Missouri at a pancake house on our way. He had fun discovering how to escape his car seat, which made the trip even more of an adventure.

Matthew's seminary was in Kirkland, about a thirty- to sixty-minute commute from our new townhouse, depending on traffic. He found some odd jobs on the side to make extra money while he was a full-time student.

Then I was hired as the director of student services for the graduate school. This was a great job for me, as I was again working with students and helping them transition to life in graduate school. I planned some special events for the students and was honored to be responsible for the commencement service. When the graduate school moved from Kirkland to Bothell, I was largely responsible for overseeing that the move went smoothly.

I had heard jokes about how when you are in graduate school and struggling financially, God seems to bless you with a child so you must trust Him on a deeper level.

That is exactly what happened. We became pregnant with our second child together. We had never really talked about exactly how many kids we wanted, but three seemed like a good number. We agreed that

I would quit work at Mars Hill and stay at home with our soon-to-be three children. Childcare for three would be out of the question for a family on a seminary budget. Matthew's school schedule was intense, so I was the main parent on duty. He helped when he could, but he also had to work some on the side to bring in some income.

I felt sad once again about not working and being with students and faculty at the school. The atmosphere there was spiritually encouraging and very intellectually stimulating. The students, staff, and faculty were a wonderful group of people who loved the Lord, and were fervently seeking to study and use their degrees to better the kingdom of God.

Champion Diers Geske blessed our family by being born on December 3, 1999. He was named after Champion Goodman Bledsoe, my maternal great-grandfather, and after Matthew's maternal grandfather, Herman Diers. We felt our family names were so special that we wanted to keep the legacy living on in the names we chose.

When Matthew graduated from Mars Hill Graduate School, he pursued a job using his counseling degree and love for the outdoors. He found a job in Gooding, Idaho at a residential treatment center for troubled youth. In 2001, we moved to Twin Falls, Idaho from Bothell.

Nine months later, he lost his job. To this day, I do not know why. He told me he and the owners of the organization did not see eye to eye on some things. Idaho is a right-to-work state so you can be released from a job with no reason given.

He took another job in Twin Falls as a counselor at a psychiatric center, but after a short stint there he decided he wanted to establish a private counseling practice.

His pattern of job restlessness and inability to stay in a job for a long period of time was starting to wear on me. I started working part-time at the College of Southern Idaho as the public information officer and contracts manager for the Office of Aging. But when Matthew wanted to pursue private counseling and become self-employed, I went to work full-time so I could carry health insurance for our family. Thankfully, my job expanded and they offered me a full-time job that included health insurance and benefits. God's grace continued to protect us.

Our marriage at this point was feeling kind of rocky. I was frustrated with all the moves and changes and the lack of stability in Matthew's work. I was taking care of three children, now working full-time, and feeling overwhelmed.

Year after year, life just seemed to get tougher relationally, workwise, and financially. I sometimes wondered, *Why did we get together in the first place?* Matthew was an introvert and I am a flaming extrovert. I felt no sense of partnership or companionship with him. I longed for a best friend, a soul mate, someone who wanted to be with me, go on vacations with me, and visit family.

Where was that friend who chatted all night with me on the bleachers when we first met? Now Matthew would plan at least a once-a-year backpacking trip with a childhood friend. If I wanted to visit my family on the East Coast I would often have to go by myself with the kids; he would either make an excuse or say he needed to work. If we had friends over, I would enjoy talking with them, while he would usually have a book in hand as if he was unaware of anyone else in the room. Matthew didn't often engage in conversation or fellowship and stayed in his own world. My loneliness felt palpable.

Our strife and contention even extended to where we went to church. We struggled to find a church where we both felt comfortable and could both grow stronger in our faith. He was more of a high-church person who enjoyed liturgy and theology with an emphasis on formality. Eventually, Matthew joined the Greek Orthodox church in our town.

I am a non-denominational kind of gal who loves modern worship. His church's love for formality and resistance to modernization contrasted with mine, an open Christian church. My church, Twin Falls Reformed Church, had vibrant teaching and incredible concert-like worship services. I even started singing with the choir at the Easter and Christmas programs.

I was spiritually being fed and growing, but not together with my husband, which I longed for. I didn't like his church and he didn't like mine. He felt I knew too many people and had too many spiritual connections. Some days it felt as if he saw my personality and desire for relationships with others as a threat and he wanted to stifle some of what God had created me to be.

Over time, we just seemed to grow further and further apart. We went to counselors and I cried out to God to help save our marriage. But somewhere on the road of life our marriage began to crumble. Our kids came first and we did not carve out time for nurturing and caring for our own relationship. We weren't following the biblical order of marriage—God first, spouse second, and kids third. We found it hard to pray together. Often, we allowed the sun to go down on our anger.

Financially, we struggled to make ends meet. Matthew would accept one job and then he would want to explore another possibility for work within a short period of time. We just did not seem to be on the same page—sometimes I wondered if we were in the same bookstore!

My husband's answer for saving our marriage was for me to join *his* church. So, for more than a year I attended his church. Instead of feeling alive, I felt like I was spiritually dying inside. The standing, incense, chanting, religious rituals, and rules were not who I was at all. There did not appear to be very much freedom in Christ in this church—or joy for that matter. My free-spirited personality and worship-leader heart died a thousand deaths every time I entered the doors of that lofty place. Trying to please Matthew, I attempted to get something out of the worship, but I left feeling empty, didn't feel close to the Lord, or that I had gotten anything out of the teaching.

One day in the spring of 2006, Matthew came to me and told me he had applied for a job online in Montana—a job where he would work for another residential facility. The residential school had invited him to come and interview for a counseling position. "This is my dream job," he said, "a chance of a lifetime I can't pass by. I feel like God is calling me to do this."

I was stunned. I felt as if someone had just kicked me in the stomach. He had never even discussed this job possibility with me prior to applying. To him this was a wonderful opportunity, but all I could see was even more division in our family. I tried to be a good Christian wife, to be obedient and compliant to his needs, so I went with him for the job interview. But deep in my heart of hearts I had absolutely no peace at all about this decision.

I just felt numb. *How can all of this be happening? This is not what I signed up for.*

After the interview, Matthew was offered the job in Montana and accepted the position. We decided I would stay in Twin Falls, work full-time, and try to keep the kids afloat in school and sports while he would live and work in Montana for a trial year.

Andrea was a high school sophomore at the time and it wouldn't have been easy for her to move at this juncture. After a year, we agreed we would reevaluate the situation. Matthew's hope was for me to find a job in Montana and relocate our family there.

Again, I did not have an ounce of peace in my heart or spirit about this decision. I felt desperate and helpless. But my husband's mind was made up; what else could I do but try to make the best of it?

June 5, 2006 was a day I will never forget. My husband pulled out of the driveway with his belongings loaded up and headed to Montana to live and be fulfilled in his "job of a lifetime," leaving his entire family behind. *What about having the family of a lifetime?* I wondered.

I remember asking God, "Can this really be your will to separate our family?" My children were filled with questions and doubts. They didn't understand why their dad had to go and wondered when they would see him again. I was left functioning as a single mom trying to balance my full-time job, parenting kids that were six, ten, and fifteen, juggling carpools, meals, laundry, and traveling to soccer games and practices.

This arrangement did not feel right to me at all. I didn't allow myself to think about where this might end up. I was raised in a family where divorce was simply not an option. In my family you got married for life and you stuck with it. You did whatever you needed to do until death called one of you home to be with the Lord. I only knew of one divorce in our family and that was a distant relative on my mother's side.

We were not divorced, just living separately. I had been left with the kids, the house, the yard, and the responsibility for all of it. It didn't take long before more resentment grew in me like a raging wildfire.

That year was a very lonely one. Matthew would come home every six to eight weeks for a long weekend to visit the kids and me. Even when he was there, we did not seem like a close family. It was as if we were playing family in a dollhouse for the time he was visiting. There was no unity or peace among us. I felt like we were plastic people who existed in different dimensions.

When he was in Montana, communication occurred mainly over the phone, and that was hard at times to keep up with because of kids' schedules and his work schedule.

The distance between us grew to the point where I wondered, *Is there another woman?*

Our marriage had not been fulfilling for years—we shared very little joy and laughter together and there was very little intimacy in our relationship. We did not often express that sense of worship and oneness that the Lord created marriage to have. The Lord has designed men and women who are married and in relationship with Him to have a passionate, fun, and enjoyable sex life. Ours felt like an obligation, like doing dishes or taking out the trash. With so many miles separating us, and infrequent visits, that intimate relationship diminshed even further.

I remained faithful—I never cheated on my husband. I prayed and believed that something miraculous would heal our marriage. Again, we went to counseling and that did not seem to do a bit of good. It seemed we would take two steps forward and then three steps backward. I just didn't know what else I could do.

During the early summer of 2007, Matthew pressed me to land a job in public relations in Montana so we could sell our house and move the family to Kalispell. I began applying for jobs there during that year, went on interviews, and tried to enjoy my times vacationing there too.

We had placed our house on the market, which I hated to do, as I loved our home, neighborhood, godly friends, and neighbors. We were so blessed where we were—I just couldn't imagine walking away. The thought of leaving this community did not seem in the best interests of our family.

The Lord seemed to close the doors to one job opportunity after another. I wondered, *Is this our plan or the Lord's plan?*

During a quiet time with the Lord, I meditated on Psalm 139:16: "All the days ordained for me were written in your book before one of them came to be." At that very moment, I felt like the Lord was speaking to me to let me know moving to Montana was another one of his doors closing. I knew in my spirit this time my kids and I were not supposed to move to Montana.

The Ministry of Angels

Friendship isn't about who you have known the longest. It is about who came and never left your side.

—Author Unknown

THOSE DAYS FOLLOWING THE accident as I lay in my hospital bed mulling over our lives together I wondered, *How can this wreck be part of God's perfect plan?*

If all the days ordained for us are written in His book, that means July 1, 2007 was part of His plan. He was with me at Milepost 95. He had not abandoned me during the accident and no matter how scary the future seemed, He would be with me then. Knowing this, while I was still lying flat on my back wondering about my marriage and future, I couldn't stay discouraged for long.

During the twenty-five days I was in two different hospitals, I was amazed at the visitors, encouraged by the prayers of God's people, and blessed by the cards of encouragement, gifts, flowers, and the sacrament of holy communion that ministered to me in supernatural ways. I felt like angels had come to visit.

When Christians follow through on those acts of kindness they feel prompted to do from the Holy Spirit, they are being obedient to what Jesus calls us to do in showing compassion and mercy to the brokenhearted.

For me these were places of "holy ground" where God and the Holy Spirit showed up in profound and real ways that brought life, encouragement, healing, and deep nourishment to my wounded soul. This healing administered to me felt like God's people were the literal hands and feet of Jesus in the flesh.

I noticed the night shift, from 11:00 p.m. to 7:00 a.m., was usually a much slower pace for nurses. They have fewer patients, and those patients obviously have to sleep, so call buttons are not pushed so frequently. Those hours became my favorite times. It was quieter, and I did not get interrupted or poked or prodded so much.

I connected with some nurses who were sources of incredible encouragement to me and ministers of prayer and refreshment. Two night nurses knew I was a Christian and that my faith, the word of God, and prayer were very important to me. After I had shared that I was a believer in the Lord Jesus Christ, this opened the door for some powerful times of conversation and sometimes even prayer. One of the nurses would even sing quietly as she picked up the room or brought fresh water and ice chips. The other one sat with me and talked when she could, and shared about her day and what she was learning spiritually in life. These were some treasured times of fellowship for sure and a distraction from the amount of pain and suffering I felt.

Natasha, another young nurse on the day shift, and I hit it off. I loved it when she worked as she had a brightness and cheeriness that was magnetic. We would laugh while she changed the bed or I would share with her some silly thing that happened during the day. She was newly married and we talked about the adjustments of marriage. She shared about wanting a family and about being a bit fearful of all that starting a family entailed.

While I was in the hospital she discovered she was expecting her first child, so I shared and celebrated this new development with her. I tried to encourage her with my pregnancy stories and what I had learned from those experiences. To this day, we are still friends and she has three more beautiful children!

In the middle of all this encouragement, my heart ached over why my husband wasn't one of the many "angels" sent to minister to me. I just didn't understand it.

Journaling each day helped me cope. As I wrote and conversed with God in words, it became a sacred time. One day I discovered I had filled up my journal—all the pages were covered with words and colored ink. I quickly sent up a prayer. "Lord, I'm asking for a journal so I can keep on writing down my thoughts and prayers."

Within a few hours, a patient-relations employee came to visit bringing me a beautiful floral journal she had purchased in the hospital gift shop. "Ask and you shall receive!" No one knew my request but the Lord, and He had heard the pleas of my heart and delivered a gorgeous journal right to my hospital bed!

"Mail time" was a joyous part of the day that I so looked forward to. I'd get piles of cards that made me laugh, and cards with prayers or a verse of scripture enclosed. The messages helped take my mind off my pain level, when the next shot was, or whether it was time for my pain meds.

One of my doctors, Dr. Cheri Wiggins, one of the main physicians on the transitional care unit, made special trips in on Sundays just to visit me. She was a southerner like me and a graduate of the University of Georgia. We had become personal friends long before she was one of my physicians.

Dr. Wiggins would bring her two-year-old daughter, Anna Grace, to see me on those lonely Sunday afternoons. That little girl had the uncanny ability to lift and cheer my spirits and I absolutely cherished those visits with Anna Grace and her mom. I'd stash graham crackers from my meals throughout the week and put them in my bedside table drawer just for her. Anna Grace would know exactly where those crackers were. She'd climb into bed with me and we would eat graham crackers together. We would snuggle and giggle and she would call me "Miss Page." To me, she was a ministering angel whose presence by my side seemed to make all my pain and heartache melt away—for a few moments.

My son David's second grade teacher, Kathy Dobbs, brought me an angel figurine that remains a permanent fixture on my bedroom dresser and symbolizes to me all the multitudes of angels that were with me during the wreck, in the ER, and then in the hospital with me each day.

Linda Baird, who had been my son Champion's first grade teacher, came by to see me one day with her daughter Tiffany Jeske, a nurse at the hospital. Tiffany said she had been in on several of my surgeries as an operating room nurse. She told me she prayed for me during those surgeries. Linda and Tiffany brought two Care Bears stuffed animals, "Cheer Bear" with its legs carefully wrapped in gauze bandages to resemble me with my two injured legs. and one with a Band-Aid on its heart, which represented Andrea and her presence in the accident.

Carol Jones, the close friend who had driven to the original hospital near my accident, took close-up pictures of my flower arrangements as they arrived in my room at the hospital and made me a journal featuring the flower arrangements on the cover. The creativity and outpouring of God's spirit through His people was like a candle He always kept lit to show me His love and concern.

Two candles in a beautiful ceramic container given to me were inscribed with the verse, "This is the day that the Lord has made we will rejoice and be glad in it" (Psalm 118:24). I was learning that whatever the day brings, I needed to rejoice and be glad in that day, regardless of my circumstances, or emotions, or the loss I was feeling.

A special verse to me then was, "The Lord is the strength of my life" (Psalm 27:1). It's one I cling to even now. In the numerous days of healing and getting better, this verse reminded me of where the strength to get better and persevere came from—the Lord!

One day the chaplains with the spiritual care team, a married couple, asked if I wanted prayer. "I sure do!" I responded. As these two servants of God prayed out loud for me I was once again encouraged by the gift of prayer as they brought me and my concerns and well-being to Jesus. Their support, compassion, and empathy helped me experience the presence of Christ through their servanthood in a way I had never experienced before.

One afternoon a petite, whited-haired woman from the spiritual care team of Ascension Episcopal Church, where we had attended a couple of years prior said, "If you'd ever like to take holy communion, I'd be happy to serve it to you." I had no idea you could request such a special thing in the hospital! "I'd love it if you'd serve me communion," I quickly responded.

As I tasted the tart grape juice and the coarse texture of the wafer, I thought of what Jesus had done for me. Not only on the cross in forgiving me of all my sins and shortcomings, but what He had done in the previous twenty days to restore my body and start the healing process. A sweet presence of God lingered over that communion and I will never forget that healing and restoring gift.

It didn't take long for me to realize it does indeed take a village to raise a child. Both my sons played on a traveling soccer team during the time of my recovery at home so there were many practices and some games I was not able to go to, yet alone drive them to. The Rapids Soccer Club of Twin Falls reached out like a family and drove my kids to and from practice and places. Each member of my "tribe" made sure my kids got where they needed to be when they needed to be there. I was in awe of the outpouring of community support.

That summer we arranged for David to go to camp at Camp Perkins, about three or so hours from our home in the majestic Sawtooth Mountains of Idaho. As excited as I was about the time away for my son to learn more about God at summer camp, I was worried. *How will I get him home from camp?* I could not drive, and was not even walking at this point. I really did not want my mom to have to make such a trek in unfamiliar territory if she did not have to.

"Lord, will you make a way to get David home from camp?" I prayed aloud.

I had the idea of sending an email to Immanuel Lutheran School, hoping there were other children from there who might be at camp that week. Maybe one of their parents could drive David home. Not long after the email went out, I got a call from Lori Jackson, one of the parents.

"I had no idea you had been in a car accident, I am so sorry. Our daughter Jennifer is up there and we need to get her so we would be glad to bring David back for you." She paused. "Now I am not sure if we are going to take the Suburban or Scott's helicopter, but one way or the other we can bring him back."

"You have a helicopter?" I asked.

"Yeah. Would that be okay if we flew him back in case we decide not to drive?"

It was all I could do to keep my composure on the phone. I am sure I said something like, "That would be fine. He'd love that! He has never ridden in a helicopter before."

I got off the phone and just had to chuckle. I had been worried that God was not going to take care of bringing David safely home to me. God, in His usual over-the-top style, had arranged a possibly once-in-a-lifetime helicopter ride back from the Sawtooth Mountains. How could I have possibly questioned the Lord's provision?

The end of David's camp week came. That afternoon the door burst open and he came running in the house hollering, "Mom, I got to ride in Jennifer Jackson's dad's helicopter! It was so cool!"

I beamed in gratitude. Isn't that just like our Lord? We pray for mere transportation and are worried about that and He answers the prayer with a plush helicopter ride home.

With this provision for my son, I had no reason to worry or question God about the rest of my life, and even the status of my marriage.

God had sent so many "angels" to minister to me while I was in the hospital. He had poured His love upon me through my unbelievable network of support.

Yet the man whose ring I wore was not present in this core circle around me.

How could my heart be so full and so empty at the same time?

That emptiness was the one thing I didn't have enough medication to numb.

The Pain That Has No Name

Good things come to those who believe, better things come to those who wait, and the best things come to those who don't give up.

—Author Unknown

THE BIG DAY FINALLY arrived—skin graft day. My legs healed very well with the use of wound care and were now ready for this next level of healing. Up to this point there had been a lot of "surgery preparation," which included pep talks by nurses and doctors. There was no turning back . . . surgery was inevitable.

Of the eight surgeries my body endured, I was most apprehensive and nervous about this one. Then Melissa, one of the nurses, said, "You might not be able to return to this particular room." My room in the transitional care unit (TCU) had been my home for almost twelve days. It was a comfy and cozy room and almost had a bed-and-breakfast feel to it—for a hospital room. When I learned that after surgery I might be transferred to another room on the same unit, my face and eyes drooped in disappointment. Just the thought of not having my familiar room to myself made my spirits sink. I felt like a torn and tattered basket that was slowly unraveling as the moments went by. The outcome of the surgery was uncertain and now I might lose my familiar room post-surgery.

I heard the nurses chattering in the hallway but couldn't make out the words. Then they came back in and Melissa said, "We've got it worked out. You can stay here." It was as if someone had waved a magic wand and granted my wish. These women believed in the importance of boosting my morale by making sure this one thing in my life remained a constant. With so many health/physical variables that were out of my control, being allowed to remain in my familiar room felt like nothing short of a miracle and a blessing. I was so grateful.

The doctor performing the skin graft surgery, Dr. Tyler Wayment, was known as a hand specialist. He had a very young-looking face, so my initial impression was to wonder, *Is a twenty-four-year-old going to do surgery on me?* He was not a tall man, but his presence, wisdom, and bedside manner seemed larger than anything in the room.

"You are in excellent hands with Dr. Wayment," I was told. "You couldn't ask for a better surgeon." I felt more at ease to have this caliber of physician putting my legs back together.

Dr. Wayment explained what was going to transpire during the skin graft surgery. The back side of my right thigh was to be the donor site. That was where the skin would be taken from and placed on my lower legs that were missing skin. The surgery involved taking a layer of the skin off the top section of the back of my leg, like a cheese slicer ever so gingerly slicing a thin piece of cheese. The section would be about ten inches long and six inches wide. Once the skin was carefully removed from the donor site it would be placed exactly on the lower parts of both calves where I needed skin so I could function in the future. Stitches would adhere the skin graft to my legs.

It was amazing for me to think that God made the human body so these things were even possible.

Dr. Wayment made it clear that the donor site area would be very sensitive and would require daily dressing changes and the stitches would need to eventually be removed. I learned not all skin graft surgeries are successful. In my case, he was looking for 100 percent acceptance of the skin graft to the open wound area.

I needed a major miracle for sure, so I enlisted prayer from friends and family. I asked them to pray for the surgery to be 100 percent successful with no margin of error. I felt confident praying for this knowing God is quite capable of answering prayer and performing miracles. He specializes in miracles!

After being in surgery for about three hours, I woke up from the anesthesia back in my "homey" room on the TCU. I was lying on my stomach as the areas that had undergone surgery could not have pressure on them or be plastered against the sheets.

When Dr. Wayment came into the room to update me, he unraveled a bit of the bandage and examined the two sites and said, "The skin grafts have taken 100 percent."

"Yay! Hallelujah! I had lots of people praying that it would be 100 percent!" I told Dr. Wayment as he stood by my side. Without thinking, I grabbed him and kissed him on the check in gratitude and appreciation. "Oh, I'm sorry!" I laughed, apologizing for being so forward.

The surgery was successful, but then came the pain. The daily dressing changes were incredibly painful as a special ointment and gauze had to be placed on the donor site to ensure proper healing and prevent possible infection. I knew the dressing changes would be bad, but wasn't prepared for how gut-wrenchingly painful they were.

Before each dressing change I had to get myself emotionally, mentally, and physically ready. I was given an anxiety pill prior to each dressing change, so I could relax while the clean bandages were applied. I normally preferred not to take medication, so it was hard for me to have to ask for a pill. But it calmed my nerves so the dressings could be changed.

One particular day, I had revved myself up for the dressing change, telling myself, *This time I'm going to be brave.*

One of my favorite nurses who was wise and kind and an amazing nurse, came into my room to do the dressing change. She began prepping the donor site to remove the gooey bandage and sticky tape. As she began lifting the bandage gingerly, right then over the intercom came, "Code blue. Code blue. All code member teams report to room 305." Someone on the unit was in far worse shape than I was. I knew code blue meant a cardiac arrest had occurred in an adult.

My nurse, who had pulled my bandage completely off, was on the code team. Per protocol, she had to leave me immediately and go assist the rest of the code team.

I lay alone with the donor site exposed to air. As the cool air in the room came in contact with the uncovered wound, it felt as if someone had thrown rubbing alcohol on my raw tissue or had taken a knife to my leg. It was horrifically painful.

I don't think my nurse was gone long, but while she was, a pool of blood started to form under my leg. I was lying in my own private blood bath on my hospital bed and it felt cold and wet.

Will the bleeding stop? I was a little afraid, but I knew my nurse would eventually come back to take care of me.

After a few minutes, the nurse came back into my room. She took one look at me and gasped, "Oh goodness, I did not mean to leave your wound exposed like that."

I tried to respond in a somewhat calm manner, and not in complete hysterics. "I knew you would be back." With my shattered hip, I couldn't move much to help myself.

"What happened at the code blue?" I asked her.

"We were able to save the person, so no life was lost; that's a very good thing."

In addition to the physical pain I was experiencing, I was keenly feeling the emotional and psychological companions to my pain. The hardest thing for me was being dependent on people and having to ask for help with practically everything. I am very stubborn and independent and before the accident had been able to do a lot of things without anyone's assistance. Now I had to ask for help to even move and get to and from the bathroom. I could not get up on my feet by myself to do anything. Once I got into the shower and was sitting on the shower chair, I could shower by myself and wash my hair. I was so grateful for every tiny area of independence!

I felt my many losses deeply. I had lost physical functioning in my legs and was not able to stand up because of my shattered hip. Until I was completely healed I was not allowed to bear any weight.

No one really knows how I feel inside, I thought in my down moments. With my reluctance to ask people for help, I wondered, *Is God breaking me of my independence?* I knew God created us to be dependent on Him and to rely on the body and community of Christ.

This was a very humbling time for me. God was at work fine-tuning my life to make me more Christ-like. While my physical body healed, He was healing me from the inside out.

I just didn't realize how painful that process could be. God's desire was for me, His instrument, made in His image, to be perfectly tuned like a beautiful harp, each string playing the sound it was intended to.

One day, Rex Lagrone, one of the managers of the IT department, rolled his wheelchair into my room, bringing me a laptop to use during the rest of my hospital stay. He is a wonderful Christian man who is highly respected in the hospital, not just for his knowledge of computers, but his knowledge of life. His sense of humor was contagious and brightened the room.

As Rex told me his story, I knew he understood loss. In his empathetic and understanding way, he told me about his tragic car accident when he was twenty-four years old. He admits it was his fault—he had too many beers before getting behind the wheel of his car and driving. The accident broke his neck and he endured a six-hour surgery that confined him to a wheelchair for the rest of his life. But that did not stop him. He went on to get his pilot's license and so did his wife, Kathy, whom he has been married to for twenty-nine-plus years.

As he talked, I realized, *He understands how I feel. He gets it!* His visit to me that day was indeed a gift from God. I began to gain a new perspective on my loss. Mine was temporary; Rex's was not. Rex would never get out of a wheelchair. I would eventually get out of my medical bed, and would graduate to a wheelchair, then a walker, and then eventually to a cane.

Rex's visit had ministered to me and blessed me in ways he may never have realized. His trauma and loss encouraged me to have a better outlook. Rex uses his injury as a platform to speak to people.

I wondered, *Will I ever be able to use my experience to help others?* The seeds of sharing my own stories to heal others began to take root in my soul.

But before I could share my story of healing, there was much more I had to endure. There were more mileposts ahead that had to be encountered.

Independent No More

I've seen better days, but I've also seen worse. I don't have everything that I want, but I do have all I need. I woke up with some aches and pains, but I woke up. My life may not be perfect, but I am blessed.

—Author Unknown

WHERE IS HE?

On July 25, my discharge day from the hospital, my husband did not come home to make sure I got out of the hospital and was situated well at home. He was in Montana at his "dream job" as a counselor to troubled youth. I think he did make the effort to check in with my mom, and may have called me once I was finally discharged from the hospital and at home that day. But it felt a little too late.

My mom, who at the time was sixty-seven years old, made all the necessary arrangements for my hospital discharge. The to-do list was longer than any laundry list for sure. Finding a vehicle that would transport me home was the first step. We needed one that was big enough and one I felt safe in as well. Given the "accident flashbacks" I continued to endure, the thought of riding in a compact car magnified my fears and created even more anxiety.

I was grateful to learn my friend Tina Phelan had a burgundy Honda van that accommodated me and all the gear I needed to bring home. I was still in a lot of pain from my shattered hip. Even riding in a van with pillows was uncomfortable. Tina drove gingerly and carefully all the way home, sensitive to any additional movement so my hip did not have to withstand more jostling.

I looked out the window as we drove home, realizing it had been twelve days since I had last been in a vehicle. The last car ride was the transport drive from Portneuf Medical Center in Pocatello to Magic Valley Regional Medical Center in Twin Falls. This was only the second car ride I had been on since the accident.

The sun was bright and warm and it felt wonderful to be out of the hospital, traveling familiar streets on the way home.

As we pulled into the driveway I felt overwhelmed with gratefulness to be home. But I was apprehensive as I thought about having to learn to maneuver around my house in a wheelchair. *How will I ever be able to do this?*

Mom had arranged for a wheelchair ramp to be placed in the garage. This was positioned from the cement floor up the two steps to the kitchen so I could get into my house. Tim Mingo, our neighbor who was known as "Tim the Tool Man" in our cul-de-sac, secured the ramp and made sure it was safe and sturdy.

Even though the ramp only covered up two steps, it felt completely insurmountable to me and as if I was climbing Mt. Everest. It seemed to take an eternity to be rolled up the ramp and into my house.

Mom had everything spotless for my homecoming. She had a medical bed set up in our den, which would become my personal infirmary. Besides the wheelchair, she had obtained a shower chair and a toilet lift, all accessories imperative for me to learn to live in my house during my healing and recuperation.

I had a lot to learn. First I had to figure out how to get into my house in a wheelchair, how to transfer to the toilet lift, and then later to get myself into the shower chair without putting any weight on my legs or jostling my painful hip. I approached it like my own personal obstacle course for the physically challenged, and felt like an Olympian when I got through.

Pip, my white bichon frisé, welcomed me home and was so glad to see me. After not seeing him for almost thirty days, it was a joy to hold and pet my little white fluff of a precious pup. My mom, who has never been much of an animal lover, had made sure Pip was groomed and looking like a shiny ball of white happiness. Growing up my sister and I could not have pets other than an occasional hermit crab, because pets created dirt and dust—two unacceptable things! Her grooming and upkeep of Pip was so thoughtful and kind and demonstrated her love for me. This probably was the one and only time that Mom had ever taken a pet to be groomed in her life!

Once I made it to my medical bed in the den, I collapsed. I felt wiped out and exhausted, both physically and emotionally. Right before my eyes closed to take a nap, Pip leaped up onto the bed and planted himself on my belly like a lap blanket of fur. It was as if he was letting me know he was not going to let me out of his sight.

Pip's nearness reminded me of the Lord's constant presence with me. He was not going to leave or forsake me. Jesus was going to be with me every step of this long ordeal called healing and recuperation.

The occupational therapist came the next day to do a "walk through" of the house, making sure I could get around safely. That whole first week was consumed with house adjustments, doctor appointments, physical therapy sessions, and meeting with the home health nurse. My mom orchestrated all the appointments, which required an immense amount of grace and patience.

In addition to all my needs, she also had the care of my seven-year-old son, Champion, twelve-year-old son, David, and seventeen-year-old daughter, Andrea. This was on top of making meals and caring for Pip and our golden retriever, Quinn.

I was back in my own home, but I couldn't vacuum, do laundry, or prepare a meal. I had to depend on my mom. For old "take charge" me, it was hard to have someone else do those things.

Mom had to make sure the boys were entertained with play dates, and were on time to soccer practices and games. Andrea had a job, but between them they only had one car, so Mom had to coordinate carpooling her to work and then arrange to get me to medical appointments. Mom also moved hoses and sprinklers, making sure our lawn was watered.

And then there was me—her most difficult charge—her medicated and moody daughter. The painkillers that eased my pain for a bit, and other medications, altered my moods and caused constipation. I had to have a daily shot of Lovenox in my stomach to help prevent blood clotting. On Coumadin, I had to be careful of the amounts of green vegetables and broccoli I ate as they interfered with how the medicine worked in my body. For a former anorexic like me who loved vegetables and broccoli, this was another difficult adjustment.

Because of the skin grafts, I had to eat a certain amount of protein each day to make sure that my skin was rebuilding and healing well. I was being told to constantly eat more, which terrified me because I could not exercise very much or walk. My old fear of becoming fat consumed me. But I had to trust the Lord with all that, because eating properly was what was going to continue to help the healing process. So I found a way to make protein shakes and eat healthy protein.

There were days when I honestly felt like the dwarf Grumpy from *Snow White* had taken over my body. I was moody and often did not feel like I had much control over it at all. I felt frustrated because I was so used to doing for others, being independent, and feeling useful. Now I was not able to do much of anything except go to doctor appointments and do physical therapy.

One day I was so frustrated by not being able to do anything that Mom and I sat on the floor and took everything out of my kitchen cabinets and rearranged them. We sorted pots and pans and plastic containers and lids just so I would feel useful. I did accomplish something. I found I had sixteen containers and only six matching lids!

The medications made me moody, tired, and irritable. I had to wear fentanyl patches, narcotic painkiller patches for my hip. One night I got so fed up with how the medicine made me feel I just ripped it off. The next morning I woke up shaking and feeling really weird.

"What did you do differently?" Mom asked me.

"I'm done with the patch. I took it off."

Mom called my pain doctor and she explained that the patches were narcotics measured out in dosages. By ripping it off I had caused my body to go into narcotic withdrawal. Even though I thought I felt bad on a low dosage of the drug, I learned going cold turkey off painkillers was even worse. I went back to wearing the patches and slowly, with the help of my doctor, weaned myself off the dosage of other medicines.

My mom is a great mom. But, as mothers and daughters do, we had our moments. We have not always agreed or seen eye to eye on things during our lifetime. When I think of her two daughters, I was the "color outside the lines" sort of daughter. I always had a lot of my own thoughts and opinions. I think often my mom did not know what to do with me. I think she must have wondered what sort of free spirit she was raising.

Mom is a person of definite opinions of how things should be: towels folded a certain way, clothes hung on the line to dry a special way, and homemade rolls only made one specific way. Those rules did not always set well with me. But there is not much my mom cannot do. She can cook, clean, drive a tractor, put up hay, and sew a dress from scratch. These qualities made her an amazing multi-tasker as she cared for me and my family.

While caring for me, I just had to let her do things the way she wanted to or needed to. There were far more serious things to worry about than whether she put dishes in the dishwasher differently than I did. I felt vulnerable and humbled by having her care for me. *This is just for a time*, I told myself. *It's not for the rest of my life.*

Friends came by to visit me and also helped transport my kids to give Mom a break. During the time she took care of me, she got to know a lot of my friends and she could see what an incredible support system I had. My friends soon became her friends and we had that in common. We'd watch movies together to pass the time and she read some of my books I had laying around the house.

When Mom and Dad made the choice that she would stay with me and my three kids while I got settled in and started the healing journey at home, I knew it was a huge sacrifice on their part. Mom stayed with me from the first week of July until the first week in October—the longest my parents were ever separated in their whole married life. At the time my parents had been married almost forty-six years. Their anniversary on August 25, 2007 was the first anniversary they had ever been apart.

I was learning the truth of what a wise person once wrote: "You spend years wishing your parents would get off your back, only to realize they are the only ones who ever really had your back."

Both my parents are my heroes; my mom for all she did to take care of me and my kids during those long, hot summer days; and my dad for making the sacrifice to be thousands of miles away from Mom. He also helped financially and gave advice when I could hardly get by from day to day—yet alone make wise decisions. I am forever grateful for these two. I see this as another blessing from a horrible accident. God used the bad to make my relationship with my parents stronger, my respect for them deeper, and my love greater.

Learning to Walk Again

Though you have made me see troubles, many and bitter, you will restore my life again; from the depths of the earth you will again bring me up.

—Psalm 71:20

WHILE OUR DEN WAS my personal infirmary and sanctuary, I learned quickly that maneuvering a wheelchair around my house was going to be challenging. It didn't take long to discover that the wheelchair worked best on the linoleum floor in the kitchen and the wood floors of the den.

I'll never look at people with disabilities the same way. I found it was no small task to get in and out of a wheelchair and move around by myself.

There was no lying around waiting to get better. The first week home I began physical therapy at the Center for Physical Rehabilitation (CPR). On my first trip to CPR, I worked hard at trying to transfer from the car to the wheelchair, balancing, getting up the sidewalk, and finding ramps into the building. I was not very patient. I decided my mom needed to be awarded a gold medal in patience and perseverance for dealing with me and my frustrations.

I had requested Julie Ellis as my physical therapist as I knew she had an incredible reputation for assisting people to return to their original quality of life as they knew it prior to an injury or accident. I knew her personally as she was a runner on the Team Weanie athletes I hung out with. Now she was going to have a different role as my physical therapist.

A few years prior to my accident we were on a women's triathlete team together: she was the runner, Beth Lamb was the swimmer, and I was the biker. We won the women's division that year mostly because Julie is an amazingly fast runner and Beth just happens to be a swim coach. Here we were a couple years later and Julie was meeting me in a wheelchair at the foyer of her therapy clinic. Things had changed just a bit.

"I heard about your accident," Julie said after greeting me. She explained I would be coming to physical therapy two to three times a week and that I would have homework assignments. "If you want to heal as quickly as possible, then it's imperative that you do the exercises to build up your strength."

I looked around at the weight machines, bikes, and every type of exercise apparatus and thought, *I can't believe I'm here. This is sure not going to be like any workout I did at Gold's Gym.* Around me were people of all shapes, sizes, and ages with injuries ranging from knee replacements to broken hips, arms, legs—you name it.

At first the therapy seemed slow and unchallenging. The exercises she had me do were with light weights, all designed to strengthen my back, core, and broken hip area.

How are these stupid little exercises and movements going to get me walking again? I fumed. I was used to a real challenge in the gym, and these small steps felt like they would take an eternity to accomplish any benefit.

Julie must have sensed my irritation and said, "This is not a quick process. It requires work, determination, and discipline on your part."

I needed to readjust my thinking. This was not a Body Pump or Pilates class. I was not going through all these repetitious exercises to burn calories and have a flatter belly and tighter abs. The goal was not to be a mean, lean, workout machine—it was to simply get stronger and eventually get to the point where I could walk without a wheelchair, walker, or cane.

Some days I questioned, *Will I ever get back to normal?*

I found that first week of physical therapy absolutely exhausting. I had to preserve my energy prior to my appointments and make sure I ate sufficient food to nourish my body nutritionally. Naps and rest and more food were on the agenda just so I could keep up the work.

Daily exercises at home were a must. I'd get on the living room floor with my blue stretchy bands and blue exercise ball and "lift, hold, and repeat" until I thought Jane Fonda was in the room running my exercise session!

"That daily homework will pay off in the long run," Julie assured me. The woman knew her stuff. I needed to do whatever Julie said to reach my full potential in healing.

The second week at CPR, a beautiful, olive-skin brunette about twenty-one years old came into the gym in a wheelchair. The therapists transitioned her onto the exercise mats for different routine exercises. I noticed the therapists were working with her a lot and wondered what her story was. Every one of us in the gym had a story that had gotten us there for exercise and rehabilitation.

I was told she had been in a car accident too, but the outcome had not been as positive for her. Her injuries had permanently paralyzed her. She would never get out of a wheelchair and she was only twenty-one. Her mother had quit her job to care for her daughter, and her family had to purchase a van equipped specifically for her wheelchair.

The words "permanently paralyzed" resounded in my mind.

Why her? Why not me? Why was she confined to a wheelchair for the rest of her life? Why was I spared that?

Yes, I was currently in a wheelchair, but I was not "permanently paralyzed."

The physicians and Julie had told me I would be in a wheelchair for a while, but then I would graduate to a walker, and then eventually a cane. When I heard this young woman's story, the little mental pity parties I had been having in my head all day seemed to dissipate. It was as if God whispered to me in a very kind and gentle voice, *Page, you will walk again; you have hope!*

I was reminded of one of my favorite quotes by Christopher Reeve, "Once you choose hope, anything is possible." My perspective once again changed. I knew I had a great deal to be thankful for. The hard work of physical therapy and home floor exercises were my road map to walking and maybe even being able to race again in the future.

Still it was a struggle to get through all the physical therapy sessions. I felt very alone. I was in a room full of people all individually working on their exercises and rehabilitating, but I had to do the work myself. No one else could help me do the hard work. I knew my future depended on my willingness to listen to my therapist, trust her, and work toward my goal.

On one of Matthew's trips home, he took me to physical therapy a couple of times. Otherwise, Mom was usually the one to take me there and pick me up afterward. One time he dropped me off, made sure I got in the building, and then went to do some paperwork for his counseling job in Montana.

He doesn't get it; he doesn't know what I am going through. I longed for him to watch a session or encourage me through difficult repetitions, but it seemed easier for him to return to his own world than try to enter my reality.

The other time that he accompanied me to physical therapy, his emotional disconnection was obvious. I needed him to cheer me on, to let me know he recognized how hard the therapy sessions were for me, and to celebrate the small victories.

That day when he picked me up afterward, he offered to take me to Costco to get us drinks. Then he suggested, "We could drive down into Centennial Park and walk around a bit and be outside." I was excited that Matthew was showing interest in something I would enjoy, being outside in the sunshine and God's creation.

"I'll take a Diet Coke," I said.

"Be right back with our drinks."

The radiant sun felt wonderful as I sat in the car with the windows rolled down.

A few minutes passed before Matthew returned to the car carrying not just drinks but some food. I was famished from the strenuous work and energy I had expended in physical therapy that morning. *Awesome,* I thought, *I'm starving. We can take the food with us to the park.*

After he hadn't shown much interest in my therapy, I appreciated his thoughtfulness to prepare me for a new challenge.

Then I noticed he had only bought lunch for himself.

"Oh, I did not know you were getting lunch stuff to take to the park," I said.

"Well, I wasn't but then when I was in there I realized I was hungry, so I decided to get something."

"Did you get anything for *me?*"

"No. I figured if you wanted something you would have told me before I went inside."

My heart sank, disappointed once again.

He's just selfish. He doesn't think about me or what I need.

I had a flashback to a couple's counseling session I had with my counselor when I was trying to work on our marriage issues. She had said, "You keep expecting he will act or respond to you in a way that is thoughtful, loving, or considerate, when he is incapable of treating you that way. You keep believing and hoping he will change for the better, when in reality, he will not change. Page, he is truly a narcissist."

I sat there with my drink in my hand while he ate his lunch, stunned that this person I was married to could not think past his own needs and consider even the most basic needs of his wife.

At that point I just wanted to go home and take a nap. But there we were at the park and I knew I'd feel uplifted and renewed out in the fresh air of God's incredible creation. So I enjoyed the scenery for a bit. Afterwards Matthew dropped me off at home and left to do paperwork or run an errand or something.

I was exhausted from the physical therapy and outing, but also the emotional encounter that had just taken place.

"Have you eaten?" Mom asked. It was around 1:30 p.m.

"Matthew got lunch for himself. He didn't ask me if I wanted any."

As Mom started making me some lunch, I thought she was going to come unglued—she too was disappointed in his behavior. She knew full well the energy toll physical therapy took on my body.

During the intense times of physical therapy and "homebound" recovery and exercises, I clung to the comfort of scripture. One of the verses that helped me was, "Be strong and courageous. Do not be afraid or terrified because of them, for the Lord your God goes with you; he will never leave you nor forsake you" (Deuteronomy 31:6).

In all the rehabilitation exercises I was going through, I knew the Lord would always be with me. His word promises He will never leave or forsake His children.

Fear would sometimes try to creep into my day-to-day routine of trying to heal and follow doctors' orders, and taking appropriate medications at the right times. I had to come against that fear with the word of the Lord: "So do not fear, for I am with you; do not be dismayed, for I am your God. I will strengthen you and help you; I will uphold you with my righteous right hand" (Isaiah 41:10).

I felt like I needed to exercise more at home, but was not sure how to go about this. Wendy Rice, who was the registered dietician who helped me learn to eat protein like a boss so my skin grafts would heal, offered to loan me her stationary bike. Wendy was an avid exerciser and runner and understood how hard it was for me not to be able to do my regular fast walking and working out at the gym.

Once we got the bike home we positioned it so it faced the French doors that overlooked my deck. That way when I was on the bike I would be able to get a view of the outside world.

I gave myself a goal of riding the bike for an hour a day. I looked forward to that hour. This was not my fast-walking routine in the canyon or using free weights in the gym, but it was a way to exercise, build strength, and get my mind off all the other things I could not do. Riding the bike was one thing I *could* do, and for that I was very grateful.

After a couple months of exercising, physical therapy, and working on strengthening my core and other limbs, the day finally came when Julie said it was time for me to begin the process of learning to walk again. My right shattered pelvis had now healed to the point that I did not have to be non-weight-bearing anymore.

I was both excited and terrified all in the same moment. *I'll be walking again!* I had started walking as a baby when I was nine months old. Here I was at forty-two years of age starting to learn something all over again that I had done all my life.

At CPR, I had big mirrors and balancing bars, instructions, and protocol—unlike when I had launched out on my first steps as a toddler.

Julie cautioned me saying, "The action of walking that felt so normal before is going to feel like a new adventure. Your brain will tell your feet to move, but it will take a while for your legs to catch up and get in sync with your brain and what your brain is telling your feet to do."

As I listened, I thought, *It can't be that bad. I've been doing this for forty-one years. It's got to be like riding a bike again.*

And then I tried to take my first step using the bars to grip for balance. The task seemed as hard as climbing a mountain. But I was determined to do whatever I needed to do to get to the end of the bars and walk on my own again.

It took many sessions with mirrors and bars and bearing weight down to relearn how to walk. It was both humbling and grueling. But, like with everything, practice makes perfect.

After I finally got strong enough, skilled, and balanced enough, I was told a walker would be my next level of independence. We secured the loan of a walker through The Wellness Tree Clinic, a medical ministry in our town. I would use the walker until I graduated to my next form of independence: a three-pronged cane.

I said good riddance to the wheelchair with glee, so happy I did not have to use that anymore and grateful for more independent mobility.

I again thought of the goodness and kindness of the Lord, who spared me from permanent paralysis. Again, not something He had to do, but something He chose to do. I remembered the words of Romans 2:4 that tell us God's kindness leads us to repentance.

The walker was a step up from the wheelchair, but it too involved a bit of a learning curve. We had to put green florescent tennis balls on the bottom of each side of the walker to make getting around easier.

The strength I had regained from all the physical therapy helped me in the times I used the walker to get to one or both of my sons' soccer games. I was so very thankful that I was alive and that I could be there to watch David and Champ play soccer.

After several weeks on the walker, my body adjusted to that and became stronger. I was then able to graduate to a three-pronged cane.

On October 3 of that year, almost exactly three months after my accident, I went back to work using a cane! It was humbling, but it was a milepost in the direction of my healing.

Will I ever be able to participate in fast-walking races again? Will I bike again? That all seemed so far out of reach. I hoped I would eventually get there. *It's in your hands, Lord, and on your timetable.*

My current assignment was to get better daily and increase my strength while trying not to look too far ahead. I didn't want to get so caught up in the future that I would miss the miracle of each moment. I wanted to see the blessings of right where God had me. I knew I had to focus on the healing occurring each day and not look weeks and months ahead.

No matter what was going on in my life, I needed to maintain an attitude of gratitude. I would need to remember this in the days just ahead.

The Severing

A man who leaves his wife with the children and the bills to go find another easier life has denied them his strength. He has sacrificed them when he should have sacrificed strength for them.

—John Eldredge, *Wild at Heart*

I saw in gradual vision, through my tears, the sweet, the sad years, the melancholy years. Those of my own life, who by turns had flung a shadow across me.

—Elizabeth Barrett Browning

WHEN MATTHEW LEFT OUR family to pursue a job in Montana without us, it was very painful for me. I felt he abandoned our marriage and family. I was left as the one to carry on with all the family responsibilities. I am a very relational person and enjoy being in a relationship and love companionship. I keenly felt the pain of being alone. I missed having him home to do daily things like go to the store together, cook a meal together, or go to the kids' activities. I did not have someone to go hiking with, go on bike rides, or for picnics.

My husband chose a job opportunity that he felt was the "opportunity of a lifetime." While his job was a professional advance and did provide more income, his absence had a negative effect on the children who were sixteen, ten, and six when he pursued the job away from home. It was clear that a hormonal sixteen-year-old girl, and two active, sports-minded boys really needed their dad to be present in their daily lives.

I was also working full-time, carrying the health insurance benefits, and trying to manage our busy children.

And, as a wife, I needed him there too. I married to share love and friendship and the actions behind his choices made me feel like an afterthought.

That whole year between June 2006 when he left and July 1, 2007, the day of my accident, took a toll on our family.

It wasn't just the little things I felt he wasn't around for, it was things that were big to me too. One year, Matthew nominated me for the "Person of the Year," a Chamber of Commerce award for my work with Safe Kids Magic Valley in Twin Falls. It was the type of affair you dressed up for—an excuse for a new dress! There was a dinner and program where we would find out the winner of this award. Once again, Matthew did not attend this event. My friend Jolene accompanied me for the evening. I did not win the award that night, but felt it was an honor to be considered.

Nobody would have given me the "Parent of the Year" award that year. I was trying to work full-time, and run a household with some semblance of meals prepared, clothes washed, and the house and yard taken care of. I had to supervise school projects, and homework, to make sure that everyone was on task. Traveling to soccer games and tournaments for the two boys had to be planned for and organized. It was a very busy time.

I worried about our daughter, Andrea, who was in her first relationship with a boy and I felt it was far from a healthy relationship. Her boyfriend was controlling, possessive, and manipulative. No amount of her words could convince me that he was God's best for her. No matter how I tried to counsel her or how many friends tried to warn her, none of it made any impact. She continued the relationship with him.

I really believe that if her dad had been around consistently during that crucial year she would have been a healthier teenager, and could have had more direction to make wiser choices. John Eldredge in *Wild at Heart* says, "A little girl looks to her father to know if she is lovely. The power he has to cripple or to bless is just as significant to her as it is to his son. If her father is passive, a little girl will suffer silent abandonment."

Although she was not in a stable relationship, Andrea was active in school, a stellar student, and was selected to go to Girl's State in Boise. That week during Girl's State, she was elected governor and legal counsel, two very important roles. Again, Matthew was not able to go with me to this prestigious ceremony; he was in Montana at his dream job that was more important than this incredible achievement Andrea had accomplished. I found a friend to watch the boys while I went to the event celebrating our daughter on my own.

That year it felt like our family and our marriage was deteriorating. I struggled and the kids struggled.

Looking back, what discouraged me the most was the thirty-six hours it had taken him to get to my hospital bedside after the accident. After that, it didn't surprise me that he didn't make any real effort to be there for me during my healing and recuperation. He was and had been alienated for quite some time, but I thought the severity of the accident would have refocused his priorities.

When Matthew did come home every four to six weeks or so for a long weekend, the dynamics would flow something like this. Mrs. Big Top Circus Leader had been running the house, disciplining, and doing the scheduling. When he arrived for a weekend, he'd want to change the way we were doing things. All of a sudden, Mrs. Big Top and Mr.

Big Top were butting heads. Then the circus animals, our three lovely children, were confused and frustrated because things had been going one way and now were changed.

I wanted everything to go smoothly, but most weekend visits would quickly turn into a tangled mess of disenchanted children and angry adults. Our experience of being in a commuter marriage/family was far from bliss.

Despite this, our plan was still for us to move to Montana so we could be together. I was supposed to be applying for jobs in Montana, and following up on the resumes I had sent out and phone calls I made so I could land a job in Kalispell.

But, in my heart, I felt reluctant. This is what Matthew wanted me to do; he felt like this was what God wanted for our family. So I, the dutiful wife, pressed on to do what he asked of me. I applied for jobs and went to interviews in Montana for various jobs, good jobs using my skills and experience in marketing, public relations, and fund-raising. But no matter how hard I tried, none of those opportunities opened up. Honestly, I didn't feel sorry that they hadn't.

One weekend I flew to Kalispell for Matthew's work Christmas party and some job interviews. The plan was that the morning of the job interviews he would escort me into town, which was quite the trek, as the cabin he was staying in was about thirty minutes from downtown. When Matthew woke up he said he didn't feel well, so he didn't go with me. I had to drive myself into town in the snow and ice and try to locate where all my interviews were to be held. I didn't have a GPS in my car and was unfamiliar with the area, so it wasn't the easiest of tasks. As I drove carefully into Kalispell, I thought, *I could really use Matthew to be here for me—and with me.* I was grateful that I made it to the interviews and got through them.

I felt as if whatever I did was never enough to get my husband's attention.

That year we spent the Christmas holiday in Montana in the little cabin in the woods that Matthew was renting. It was a far cry from Bing Crosby's "White Christmas" with happy people breaking into song. Oh, it was white—there was plenty of snow—after all it was Kalispell in northern Montana and close to Canada. But the kids really wanted to be at our house with their own belongings and their own traditions. The atmosphere was tense. We couldn't agree on things, and there was a sense of disappointment among the kids. That Christmas did not go down as our best one ever.

I did not wake up one morning with the revelation, "I think I will go and get a divorce today." Each person goes through their own individual journey to get to the place where he or she realizes the marriage cannot survive.

A pivotal time for me came when my parents sat me down at my kitchen table. Dad had flown out to see me again the summer of the car accident. "Page," he said, "Mom and I don't feel you are being treated well, emotionally, physically, or spiritually. We're concerned about your marriage."

This was coming from two people who were close to celebrating their forty-sixth wedding anniversary. They had been around both the life and relationship block.

"We don't feel like you are really in a relationship at all," he added. Tears welled up in my father's eyes and his hands trembled as he spoke those words.

Right then, something settled in my heart. *I knew.* I knew it might be *socially* possible for me to get out of this "marriage." It might be OK.

Obviously, divorce is not what God would choose for any of us. In my case, it seemed like severing this relationship for good might be the best thing for me as well as the kids. I had long wrestled with these thoughts in my head. What my parents told me echoed my own thoughts.

I felt I needed to take some action and realized it was time to consult an attorney.

I talked with my friend Tina who had been through a divorce and knew how to maneuver difficult waters. This was completely uncharted and unfamiliar territory for me. I felt as if I was in a rowboat approaching the perfect storm and I did not want to capsize.

"I'll go with you to the attorney; in fact, I'll take you there," Tina said. I could count on her for emotional support. I was still in a wheelchair at this point and felt very vulnerable both physically and emotionally.

I made an appointment with a Christian attorney who was a straight shooter who would be open and honest with me and would look out for my best interests and those of my children. I had started down the road to divorce.

Since I was still in a wheelchair, we had to call prior to my appointment to determine the best place to park that was handicap accessible. Tina arrived in her burgundy Honda van and helped get me situated into the vehicle for transport to the attorney's office, and we were on our way.

I was an emotional wreck that morning. Nervous about the appointment, my head was full of questions and concerns as I thought about what was ahead.

As we entered the building, the secretary greeted us. She was a friend of a friend and had also recently been divorced so I knew she understood how I felt, which was comforting. I needed that bit of comfort. As Tina helped maneuver me into the attorney's office I felt jittery and shaky. I kept thinking to myself, *Am I really going to do this? Am I going to file for divorce? This is absolutely nuts!*

The attorney's walls displayed lovely pictures of his daughters and wife. I had worked with him on several projects through work and knew his wife.

As the meeting started, I expected I might get a lecture from Mick. Would he say, "Are you really sure you want to go down this road?" Would he give me a list of reasons why I should not pursue divorce?

But my attorney looked at me with a fatherly look and said, "I have heard that your husband has not been treating you very well from numerous people. What took you so long to get to this point?"

Immediately relief flooded my body. I felt my nervousness and doubt dissipate and a wave of peace go through me. *He understands. He gets it.* Obviously, he had heard from some of our mutual friends about the far from compassionate ways I was being treated by Matthew.

It confirmed I was not making this stuff up or exaggerating; I truly was in a very unhealthy marriage. I was not adored, cherished, treasured, cared for well, or at all. This was not how marriage was supposed to be. God intends for marriage to be much healthier. The verse, "A cord of three strands is not quickly broken," (Ecclesiastes 4:12) was not occurring in our marriage. After thirteen years of marriage, the adoption of our daughter, birthing and raising two sons together, I was filing for divorce.

My attorney friend told me he had a conflict of interest handling my divorce as he was applying for a judgeship in a different city. But he gave me some wise counsel and recommended some other divorce attorneys in the area. He walked through a little of what I could expect in the upcoming weeks of filing for a divorce. "Everything will be okay; you'll make it through this," he reassured me.

After a second round of lawyer research I retained an attorney from a local law firm in town and went through all the necessary legal paperwork to file for divorce.

Thanksgiving was coming up and we had planned to be together for the holiday. I thought, *This will be our last holiday as a family*. I didn't want Matthew to be served his divorce papers until after that gathering.

Matthew called me on the phone saying, "I don't want to come to Twin Falls. I don't live there anymore." He said he'd fly into Boise, which is about a two-and-a half-hour drive from our home in Twin Falls. "I'd like you to bring the kids down there on Thanksgiving Day and we'll stay in a hotel for the weekend." This would be more convenient for him as he would not have to make the two-hour trip from Boise to Twin Falls and then back to Boise to fly back out after the holiday weekend.

I did not like his idea for the Thanksgiving weekend at all. Thanksgiving was supposed to be spent at home or with family or friends, not in a hotel room in another city where we didn't have family or friends around. But I knew I had to abide by his wishes and do what he suggested or we'd be in another huge fight.

"I'll be flying in late on Thanksgiving Day." He expected me and the kids to pick him up at the airport when he got in. When I found out his flight schedule I realized the kids and I could stay in town and have a somewhat traditional Thanksgiving dinner with our friends the O'Connell/Jacques family who we had spent Thanksgiving with for years.

Thanksgiving Day came and the kids and I had our usual day with our friends. Then we headed to Boise to pick up Matthew and spend the rest of what was left of the day with him in a hotel.

We made the trip in my new vehicle, a light blue 2006 Toyota Highlander. When our Pilot was totaled in the accident, we got $8,000 to put down on a replacement vehicle.

The purchasing of a replacement vehicle was yet another source of contention in our marriage. Matthew had his thoughts and I had mine, and we could not agree. I wanted another small SUV-type vehicle because of safety concerns, and I also felt like I could see better and was safer higher off the ground. He dismissed my feelings and thought we should get a regular Honda car. This time, I did what I thought was right and bought the car I felt safe in, the Highlander SUV.

After the kids and I got to Boise, we picked their dad up from the airport. I noticed he seemed unusually stressed and was acting a bit odd. As he got in the new vehicle, he immediately voiced his disapproval over my choice in cars.

At the hotel where we would spend the weekend, he said he was hungry and needed something to eat. We were all still full from our Thanksgiving dinner and the kids were tired from traveling, so we stayed in the room while he ventured out to find some food.

"I didn't even get to have Thanksgiving dinner," he said before he left. I thought, *This is ironic. It was your idea not to have a traditional holiday at home.* He came back with some food and visited with the kids a bit and then we settled in for the night.

That night he made no moves toward any type of intimacy; no hugging or embracing—nothing really. That was okay with me, but not his usual behavior. That weekend he slept in one of the queen beds with one of the boys, I was in the other bed, and Andrea was on a pull-out in our room.

The next morning Matthew surprised me when he announced, "This is my weekend with the kids since I haven't seen them. I'll let you know what meals and activities you can be a part of."

This is really weird, I thought as he outlined the rules for the weekend. *I don't think he knows I am filing for divorce. Why is he acting so weird?* It didn't look as if this was going to be the one last "normal" family holiday weekend together I was hoping for before everything changed.

That whole weekend I drove him and the kids to wherever *he* wanted to go—meals, the park, whatever, and then he dictated if I could be a part of the activities or not. If I wasn't included, then he called me to come pick them up when they needed a ride.

Inside I was a mess knowing he would be served divorce papers once he got back to Montana. Strangely, he was already treating me like an ex-spouse, letting me know when I could and could not be with our kids and him. It was all very awkward.

I wondered why he was acting so distant; it was hard to fathom. *Has Matthew met someone else?*

When I saw Matthew's phone on the table, I picked it up and checked the call history. On Thanksgiving Day there were eight calls to a single number in Montana, the day he was traveling to meet us.

I confronted him. "I looked at your phone, Matthew. You've got all these calls to one number. What's that about?"

"That's just another counselor I'm working with. We've got clients we're working together on. I needed to talk to her about some treatment plans."

Eight calls on Thanksgiving Day—really? All of this was hard for me to believe. Coupled with how weird and even more distant he was acting, I couldn't help but wonder. He also was renting a room in the home of this woman and her husband. Besides the eight phone calls, he was acting so disconnected and obviously did not want me around.

It was time for us to drive back to Twin Falls for the school and work week ahead of us. The good-byes were tense and awkward, just like the entire weekend had been. Matthew was leaning into the car saying good-bye to the boys when all of a sudden something switched in him.

He took off his wedding ring and threw it at me, yelling, "This is not really a marriage anyway. You don't seem to want to be married—so here's my ring!" He slammed the car door and walked away.

Shocked that he had acted this way in front of the children, I was not sure what to do. I picked up the ring and walked back into the hotel to give it back to him. He was just going into the room when I caught up with him. I handed it to him and he took it, but then slammed the door in my face.

I just stood there stunned in the hotel hallway. A moment later, he opened the door and threw the ring back at me and slammed the door shut again.

That is how our family Thanksgiving weekend ended. If I ever needed confirmation I was doing the right thing, that moment was it.

Before going back out to the car, I tried to gather my composure. I knew I would have to talk to the kids about this embarrassing outburst. I don't even remember what I said to their questions of, "Is Daddy mad?" and "Are you fighting?" I tried to reassure them that everything was going to be all right.

On the two-and-a half-hour drive home, I felt numb; yet a sense of peace settled in my heart. *Filing for divorce was the right thing to do. This is not a loving marriage at all.* It was obvious that Matthew did not want to be married anymore either. I didn't know if he would admit that or even be in touch with his feelings enough to admit that.

Back home in Twin Falls, I knew the next couple of weeks would be rough. Matthew would be served divorce papers, and of course, there would be ramifications from that.

I thought back to a time during the previous summer when Pastor Patrick O'Grady, Matthew's Orthodox priest came for a visit to our house. He had been aware of how splintered our marriage was and we started talking about divorce. He said, "If you are thinking seriously about this, you need to make sure your reason for divorce is biblical."

"Isn't adultery the only biblical grounds for divorce?" I asked.

"There is another verse that I feel fits your circumstances," Father Patrick said. He quoted, "Anyone who does not provide for their relatives, and especially for their own household, has denied the faith and is worse than an unbeliever" (1 Timothy 5:8).

I thought about this scripture, but at the same time I knew it was not God's first desire for people to divorce. I knew what scripture said in Malachi 2:16: "For I hate divorce," says the Lord, the God of Israel." But I read and reread the verse Father Patrick shared with me.

This has happened in our marriage. Matthew left us. Spiritually, I felt better about contemplating divorce. Up until this point, it had been like a furious ping-pong tournament going on in my head. With the clarification from God's word and this pastor as well, after some time, I knew my decision was for the right reasons.

For me divorce seemed inevitable. Obviously, divorce is not the answer for everyone. God can reconcile relationships, heal and restore marriages, and that is a wonderful thing. It did not seem that our marriage would be restored and the relationship reconciled.

We were going in two different directions spiritually and professionally. Matthew seemed to be at peace and content in the church he had found, but it was not the place where I felt I could grow. I needed a church that had meaningful worship and teaching and small groups that ministered to my soul. He was very committed to working in the outdoors with troubled youth, while I felt the Lord had made it clear that I needed to stay where I was professionally.

My hope and prayer through all of this was that I would emerge a better and stronger person. Stronger in the sense of being able to push through this difficult decision and make sense of what it would mean to be divorced and officially be a single mom. I was determined to press into the Lord and His strength and His Word.

My divorce took an entire year to be finalized. There were issues of finances, custody, and visitation, all those things that are the normal part of ending a marriage. Since Matthew was living out of state, I was given residential custody and the kids would be with me through the school year. They would spend eight weeks during the summer with him, including long school breaks. Christmas vacations were divided in half. Every other Thanksgiving holiday they were with me.

The boys' birthdays are in June and December, so many times they were with me. If not, we made sure we had a party or celebration either on or around their birthdays. We agreed that Father's Day would be spent with him and Mother's Day with me.

We were required to attend court-ordered parenting classes. Fortunately, since we lived in different cities and states, I did not have to attend these alongside Matthew.

These classes were some of the least desirable aspects of the whole divorce proceeding. Some parents argued publically and used profanity. It made me wonder why there are not major requirements before a person can become a parent. Just simple things like providing shelter, food, and clothing seemed like huge obstacles to many in these classes. Some appeared rough around the edges; their priorities seemed to be piercings, tattoos, and manicured nails and toes. I wondered if they were providing emotionally stable environments for their children.

Our kids were required to go to age-appropriate classes while I was in my class. There they processed what was going on with a counselor trained to help kids navigate the muddy waters of their families dissolving. I remember the boys had to read, *Dinosaurs Divorce*, a simple book that explained through the eyes of a dinosaur family how this affects everyone in the family.

Since their dad was in another state, I was the main parent to help them work through their issues and questions. I was grateful the boys did not have to split their weeks up going back and forth from one parent's house to another, or even every other week. As I listened to the other parents in class, I was grateful for the consistency in our visitation schedule. I thought that would help with schooling and maintaining lasting friendships for the boys as well.

In any divorce, there is splitting up of furniture and belongings. Those are truly just objects when you look at the big picture of the real loss of relationship and family that takes place.

I decided to keep the house and to write Matthew a check for the equity and the balance of the belongings that I owed him for. I had just gone through a year and a half of eight surgeries and learning to walk again. I was just starting to get full mobility. The thought of uprooting and finding another place to live just did not seem right. There had already been loss—tremendous loss for me—physically, emotionally, relationally—but there was huge loss for the children as well. I thought it was the right thing to keep the house, and our neighborhood, neighbors, and schools as a constant.

In retrospect, I probably should have sold the house and downsized a bit and made things a little simpler. After I decided to keep the house, the economy tanked and my house depreciated in value even more. But the consistency of staying in our home and neighborhood was a positive for us. The boys flourished both socially and academically so I feel "staying put" and keeping their home and neighborhood the same was a good decision.

Wonderful neighbors and friends saw us through that time and continued to be anchors in the storms of life. We processed a lot of grief. Sometimes it felt like peeling an onion, one layer at a time. Isaiah 61:2 comforted me with the words, "To comfort all who mourn, and provide for those who grieve in Zion." That is who our God is and He was with us every step of the way.

After the divorce, I was advised to go through a course at our church called DivorceCare, a fourteen-week, biblically based course to help make sense of the "new normal" of divorce. Every Monday night I would figure out childcare and head to my class, and I'm so glad I did. The classes touched on everything from finances, parenting, and sex after divorce. The instructors were Patti and Al Rohweder who were phenomenal leaders. Since then Patti and I have become biking buddies.

One of the helpers in the class was Jennifer, a friend of mine who had been married to an alcoholic and was a single parent. I was encouraged to see she had not only survived her divorce but was thriving, growing in Christ, and giving back to the body by serving in this class. God had done a tremendous work in her spiritually and emotionally. I longed for that healing to transpire in my own life.

Our divorce was final on October 30, 2008.

"Plan a getaway during that time," a wise friend told me. "You need to celebrate the ending of one chapter and beginning of another." I prayed long and hard about what to do and where to go.

I felt God was encouraging me to go see my friend Leslie (Grant) McClure in Chino Hills, California. I would use a plane ticket voucher from the year before that I needed to use before it expired. Leslie was ecstatic to hear I was coming. On October 31, I flew out to California. My kids were with their dad for the weekend so I was free to go.

Leslie is one of my F.R.O.G friends (Fully Reliant on God) along with Carol Jones, the friend who was the first person to visit me at the trauma center in Pocatello after the accident. At least once a year we'd get together for a visit of spiritual encouragement and laughter. Leslie used to live in Twin Falls, so when we all lived in the same town we got together more frequently. After her move to California, our visits became yearly. We'd even give each other gifts with a frog motif in keeping with being Fully Reliant on God women.

Leslie will understand where I am right now. She too had been divorced and had been a single parent raising four kids. At the time of my divorce she had been married two years to David McClure, who she had met on a dating site called Christian Mingle, and had moved to California. The couple had one son at home, Leslie's from her previous marriage, and she was helping to raise David's sons. David's wife Cynthia had passed away several years before from cancer and had left him as a single parent.

Leslie is like a big sister I never had. She is seven years older—and seventy years wiser! She has always been someone I could text or call or email when I needed prayer, a shoulder to cry on, or a good laugh to help me get through a situation.

At the airport, it felt as if no time had passed since we had last seen each other. We just picked right up where we left off in our friendship and conversations. Leslie and I headed straight to a Halloween store to purchase masks for the dinner theatre we would be going to that night. I picked out a butterfly mask as I love butterflies and have a whole bathroom in my house completely decorated in butterflies. They had become symbols of my new life and how Christ can make all things new again! At the dinner theatre, we had a wonderful time laughing and enjoying the show. I think we laughed so much that our crow's feet had baby crow's feet around our eyes!

The next day Leslie had planned a little excursion to Huntington Beach. We had a lovely walk on the beach in the warm sun, ate seafood at a beachside restaurant, and stayed in a beautiful stone hotel with a castle theme.

In the gift shop of the hotel, I checked out the jewelry display. A sterling silver ring in the shape of a crown caught my eye, so I asked the lady behind the counter if I could try it on.

"What a beautiful ring," I said.

"Yes, it's like a princess ring!" the saleslady said.

For almost fourteen years, I had worn a wedding ring. I thought about how naked my ring finger had been feeling without my ring—and how charming this crown ring was.

A wedding ring symbolizes relationship, a tie to another—a sacred commitment. It signifies identity of being married, taken, spoken for.

I stood at the counter looking down at the silver crown on my finger and thought about my new identity. In the quiet of the moment, it was as if the Lord spoke to me in a whisper, *Page, you are a daughter of the King; you* are *a princess.*

I bought that inexpensive silver ring and wear it with pride on my left ring finger.

As I embraced my new identity fully, it became part of my healing process. It felt as if I had reached yet another milepost as I came to grips with my identity in Christ as a divorced woman.

When people notice the uniqueness of the ring or make a comment about my "crown ring" I have an opening to share that I am indeed a "daughter of the King," and that my identity is in Christ. I am not married to a person, but I am a bride of Christ and married to Him.

Many people over the years have asked me about my crown ring and where they could get one. I've then shared with joy a bit of my story, and also about Christ who is the King of kings and Lord of lords and how He has healed me.

Doing Life Together

Friends are quiet angels who lift us to our feet when our wings have trouble remembering how to fly.

—Lorainne K. Mitchell

Carry out a random act of kindness, with no expectation of reward, safe in the knowledge that one day someone might do the same for you.

—Diana, Princess of Wales

I TRULY BELIEVE WE don't meet people by accident. They are meant to cross our path for a reason. After the divorce, I knew I needed the healthy support of friends.

When my dental hygienist, Lorinda, learned about my car accident and subsequent divorce, she told me about her small group at my church. Heart to Heart was a group of four women who were divorced or remarried and who supported one another and spent time together.

Lorinda talked to this group to see if I could visit and possibly join. I was thrilled when the women made an exception for me and turned it into a group of five. These women "did life" with me during a very painful and difficult time in my life, and for that I am forever grateful.

One day when my mom was still living with me and helping me to get back on my feet physically, we went to the mall for an outing as I was going stir crazy in the house. I was still using my walker, and not the fastest shopper on the block.

"Mom, go do your own thing. I'll hobble around on my own. Meet me in The Little Red Hen." This was one of my favorites and one of the best gift shops in town. It was full of Vera Bradley items, pottery, nativity scenes, quote plaques, candles, chocolate—you name it, this store has it.

As I slowly made my way into The Little Red Hen on my walker, a petite store clerk wearing an apron and something purple put her hands on her hips and exclaimed, *"What in the hell happened to you?"*

That was my introduction to Cindy Juker who soon became one of my best friends. I gave Cindy the *Reader's Digest* version of the accident.

That day when I met Cindy I didn't know she was in Lorinda's Heart to Heart group. She was one of the women who I had heard about at my teeth cleanings over the years. Cindy was divorced and not remarried, worked for the Department of Health and Welfare for years, and her office was in the same building where my office was located.

One of the most creative women I have ever met, Cindy is a total "decorator diva." During the Christmas season she has at least nine trees decorated by theme—a nativity tree, a s'more tree, an outdoorsy tree, and on and on. When you visit during the holidays it's as if you've walked into the downtown Chicago Macy's with the trees, her ornate Christmas village, and the smells of fir candles and chocolate. Serious Christmas blitz! She lives the message of the picture she hangs above her tree—"Keep Christ in Christmas!" That's my Cindy—love, love her!

Shelly McElliott is another one of the Heart to Heart members who is also very artistic by nature. If there is anything to do with art or computers she can do it. She is divorced and I think her favorite title is grandma to her three grandchildren.

Kathleen Atwell, another member of the group, is remarried to Verlyn Broek. She is a nurse by profession, one of the sweetest women on the planet. Her husband is my eye doctor, and he's a pilot so she is often out and about on excursions with him.

God created the body of Christ to function in community—for us to be there for each other in a myriad of circumstances. These women brought me a rare and precious sense of a loving and supportive community. I am so grateful for their presence in my life that has been a healing balm over the years.

This small group was not a formal Bible study group. We didn't meet each week and do a hermeneutical study of a passage in the Bible. Nor did we do a book talk. I would call this group of women the "Getting-Through-Life Girl's Group." When situations came up in one of our lives, we were there to pray for and be *who* we needed to be for each other.

After my divorce, I needed to go through boxes of things unclaimed by my former husband and figure out what I wanted to keep or give away. One day my Heart to Heart group came over to my house to help me sort, keep, or toss belongings. While we were doing this tedious task, Cindy got a call from her older daughter Paula who was in the U.S. Army.

The expression on Cindy's face told me this was serious. We gave her as much privacy as we could in a garage full of plastic totes and chatty women. When she got off the phone she said, "There's a pretty strong possibility that Paula will have to be deployed overseas."

This was several years after 9/11 and America was involved in the War on Terror. Paula was then a single parent of one very active little boy, Jordan. If she was indeed deployed, Jordan would have to go live with Paula's mother Cindy, and her dad, David, while she was overseas. It was not ideal for her as a single parent to leave her only son and go fight in another country, but that was what Paula had signed up for when she chose to serve our country and fight for our freedom.

As Cindy shared with us, the task we were doing seemed trivial and meaningless in comparison to the news. Right then, we all stopped sorting and labeling and gathered in a circle, held hands, and prayed out loud in my garage. Mainly we prayed that Paula would *not* have to be deployed this time.

It was wonderful and powerful to be in a group of women who were sold out to the Lord, committed to what it really means to be in community, and most importantly committed to prayer.

Those prayers were answered as Paula did not have to be deployed.

Even though I am the daughter of a botanist, this does not mean that I can grow anything green, keep an immaculately landscaped yard, or know how to properly prune anything. Cindy has the gift of growing things, making yards look lovely, and pruning. She has even been caught a couple of times pulling weeds in a ditch along the highway!

Cindy came over one day to help me chop a honeysuckle bush down in my front yard. I usually pay her in food, so we would share a meal together and talk after we worked. This bush had roots that were about three inches in diameter. Cindy then trimmed my umbrella trees that were about to take over my flower beds. With the pruning shears in her hands, in no time those umbrella trees were in tip-top shape.

One year we took some old windows that had been torn out of an old restroom at the Twin Falls County Fair Grounds, sprayed the frames with green paint, and installed them on the shed in my backyard. Thanks to Cindy, my shed looked like a cozy little cabin.

One fourth of July, Cindy and I took her tent, known as the "Juker Inn," to camp at Magic Mountain, a nearby recreation spot in the South Hills mountain area. This tent is one of the coolest on the planet with its front screened area I called the front porch. It reminded me of one of my favorite bed and breakfast places in Black Mountain, North Carolina, The Red Rocker Inn, a place with a spacious, sprawling front porch with charming red rockers.

We packed up as much stuff that would fit into my Highlander and headed to the beautiful South Hills, about a fifty-minute drive from Twin Falls. Located on National Park Service land, it was a haven in winter for skiing and snowmobiling, and a camper's wonderland and all-terrain vehicle destination in summer.

We spent that long weekend camping, reading, and eating good meals. I'd wake up to the aroma of Cindy's camp coffee, and later we had her to-die-for Dutch-oven chicken. That summer was a beautiful warm one in Idaho, which means not much rain and a ton of dirt since we're in high desert terrain. After a few days of being outside in the heat with no showers, we came home happy but with our clothes ingrained with dirt—and we learned from this to never wear your good Victoria's Secret bras camping as that is why sports bras were created.

After I had advanced to where I did not need my walker anymore, I made a choice to venture out and do some things outside—to use God's incredible creation as an atmosphere for more healing. It had been quite a long transformation physically, but I was so grateful to have gained my mobility back.

One of the adventures the small group attempted twice was kayaking and canoeing the Snake River, one of my fondest memories. Lorinda and Alan, her new husband, were in a canoe. Kathleen and Verlyn were in a tandem kayak. The rest of us, and Krystal, Cindy's college-age daughter, made up the remainder of the motley kayaking crew. There was abundant laughter and lots of splashing and fun. We went from Centennial all the way to Pillar Falls and then got out and walked around on the rocks there. I've never laughed so much or had so much fun in water and boats on the Snake River in all my life. There was such a caring spirit present in our group and we all just really enjoyed each other's company. Fun friends and great personalities equal wonderful memories.

Once a year, we tried to organize a hike up to Pioneer Cabin in the Ketchum/Sun Valley part of Idaho. Cindy's nephew Sam allowed us to camp out in his condo there. We'd usually make a morning trek to Starbucks for a cup of joe before hitting the scenic trail to Pioneer Cabin. This is a pretty steep hike that can only be done in the late spring, summer after the snow melts, or early fall before the snow starts descending on the beautiful Sawtooth Mountains.

The trail meanders for more than seven miles, round trip, of amazing scenery and countryside. If we timed our hike just right, we'd see a magnificent carpet of colorful wildflowers along the path. I was upright and walking on my own, without a walker or a cane. It was incredibly humbling to realize how the Lord had restored my health so I was able to do such a strenuous hike.

I had come a long way from the day of the crash at Milepost 95.

The first time we hiked to the cabin it had rained and then snowed on us as we reached the top with the cabin in clear sight in the distance. As we got closer to the cabin we could read the sign on the top that says, "The higher you get, the Higher you get." Dressed in shorts, we were thankful we had brought sweatshirts with us, just in case. Idaho weather can change quickly.

The now abandoned two-room Pioneer Cabin, built by the Sun Valley Company during the summer of 1937 as a ski touring hut, has a heavy, steel woodstove and metal bunk beds, a table, and a couple of chairs. Once we arrived at the cabin at 9,500 feet elevation, we drank some water and ate a granola bar for nourishment on the trek back down the mountain.

I looked around the small cabin at the notes that people from all over the world have written and left on the table or nailed to the walls. Picking up a pen, tears filled my eyes as I wrote a note of gratitude for my ability to walk to Pioneer Cabin. I had much to be thankful for indeed. There were times after the accident when I doubted I would ever be able to hike again. This was one adventure I did not take for granted.

While our little group was enjoying a wonderful time of fellowship and soaking in the beauty of the wildflowers and the views from the mountain, we spotted a shabby and rustic-appearing Basque sheepherder descending the mountain with his sheep. I didn't know where he had come from or where the herder and his sheep were going, but we watched as the sheep followed and obeyed him. They seemed to know their lives were in the hands of the herder and that they needed to stay close to him, as without him they would be lost.

I thought about how we are like sheep as followers of Christ. He tells us, "I am the good shepherd. The good shepherd lays down his life for the sheep" (John 10:11). And, "My sheep listen to my voice; I know them, and they follow me" (John 10:27). On that mountaintop that day, I was grateful I could hear my Shepherd's voice and follow Him, wherever He might lead in the future.

During the time our small group was together, Shelly was divorced for the second time. We rallied around to support her as well as pray for her health issues. Lorinda had met the man of her dreams, Alan Horner, while our group was together. Cindy hosted a lovely bridal shower at her home where we had a great time. Kathleen and Verlyn had been the ones to initially set Lorinda and Alan up on a date.

Kathleen's sister-in-law was diagnosed with cancer. Again, we prayed and supported Kathleen and her family. Kathleen, a nurse by profession, was a wonderful blessing to her sister-in-law during her journey with cancer. Kathleen went along on a family sailing trip that was one of her sister-and-law's final wishes, to administer medication, healing words, and prayers during her final days.

Cindy, Lorinda, Kathleen, and I started walking the canyon together for exercise and fellowship. We nicknamed ourselves the "Walkie Talkies" because we talked and walked together.

During the course of our relationship, both Cindy's daughters were married. Lorinda accompanied Cindy on the road trip to California to help with one wedding. Kathleen's daughter was recently married in a beautiful outdoor wedding at Pillar Falls, and both Cindy and Lorinda helped with this celebration.

God gives us people in our lives at just the right time—when we need them. He is never too early or too late. His timing is impeccable. The women in this group were there for me during a tough season in my life and they have been there for me during some happy times as well.

They have been like fresh, white snowflakes in a long, dreary, gray, windy Idaho winter. They have been the gorgeous yellow and tangerine tulips that bloom in the spring. During the summer, they have been the refreshing, babbling brook in a hot and dry desert. And, during the fall, they have been the vibrant, crisp leaves that brighten a trail in the woods. I am so grateful they welcomed me into their group at a time when I desperately needed all of them. My life is much richer because of the like-minded women who supported me through both rough and smooth waters.

The community of committed friends who loved me at different times in my life has been yet another significant milepost in my journey.

Walking for Life

Strength of character isn't always about how much you can handle before you break. It's also about how much you can handle after you've been broken.

—Robert Tew

SEVERAL YEARS PRIOR TO the car accident, some of my athlete friends on my Falls Brand Team Weanie introduced me to the Sawtooth Relay, a sixty-mile relay run with five teammates. The intense course, always the second Saturday in June, begins in Stanley, Idaho, north of Sun Valley in a gorgeous section of the mountains and ends in Ketchum, Idaho. The route goes up and over Galena Summit, a high mountain pass in central Idaho at an elevation of 8,701 feet above sea level.

I am a fast-walker so I have either been on a team of all walkers or on a mixed team with walkers and runners every year. Just prior to my car accident on July 1, 2007, I had completed this challenging relay in June.

In 2006, my team won second place in the coed mixed master's division made up of both runners and fast-walkers. This was one of my greatest achievements as a fast-walker. The relay consists of twelve legs;

each person does two legs, a total of about ten or so miles altogether, but never back-to-back. I did leg two and then leg eight. The break in between the race legs allows your body to get restored and recover from the first leg, and from the elements. Even though the relay is in June, it can snow, sleet, hail, or be 85 to 100 degrees.

The summer of 2008, one year after the accident, I was still recovering from the surgeries and gaining my strength back. I was trying to build up my walking endurance.

In 2009, I felt I had healed enough to take a leap of faith, so I registered for the Sawtooth Relay joining Cindy Juker, Cindy Collins, Kathy-Stuart Williams, Tina Brandt, and Crystal Greene.

The relay is not just about a race—it is about the journey and experiences along the way that build community and friendship—and the memories that can never be taken away.

The pre-race fun begins when you drive to Ketchum and stay in a motel room together. And then you travel to the race start, which is in Stanley, about a fifty-minute car ride away. We drove the very sixty miles that our team would be walking once we reached Stanley and started the relay. Your vehicle of choice is your "encouragement mobile." While each person is racing, the rest of the team keeps the times and either is getting ready for their next leg or recuperating from the leg they may have just completed.

Crystal Greene's husband, Bill, has been the backbone of the Falls Brand Team Weanies and packs more into a day than most people half his age. On top of working full-time, he always made time to send out weekly emails to our Weanie team, letting us know about upcoming races and race results, and making sure that people knew their finishing times from races.

After a night of no sleep in the hotel, I was nervous and apprehensive about making this attempt. Besides dealing with my own fears, I did not want to let these women down and disappoint anyone because of my poor performance. I picked legs two and eight for this first post-accident relay. I knew what to expect on the course, one variable I could have a little control over.

Being on a walking team meant our group started around midnight so walkers wouldn't be in the way of the runners when they came through. At about 10:30 or 11:00p.m., we headed to Stanley and checked ourselves in at the race start, making sure we had at least two reflective vests and two head lamps for walking in the dark. The first four runners/ walkers would most likely be doing their part of the race in the dark.

We started the relay with pictures of the group and words of great encouragement to the first one on the course—Tina. She is a fast, strong walker and completed her leg in record time. Now it was time for me to be in the waiting area for her to hand off to me as I would follow her. Nervous about how my body and legs were going to do, I plugged in my worship tunes and started leg two.

It was dark and I could hardly see where I was going in the light of my headlamp. I planted my feet carefully each step, concerned about falling and breaking something else. I had some fear of breaking another bone, or ending up injured and having to undergo more pain and a setback in my health, so I was probably overly cautious as I walked the course.

During my leg of the race, I thought about the privilege of being able to walk again. *Lord, it's only your goodness and mercy that my legs were spared in the accident.*

When it was my turn to do my second leg of the day, leg eight, praises to God welled up inside me. *Thank you Lord for my life. Thank you for all you have done to heal me so far.* I remembered reading the words of Jeremiah 30:17: "'I will restore you to health and heal your wounds,' declares the Lord."

As I rounded a bend on the downside of Galena Summit, I glanced up and saw Cindy Juker taking pictures. I had a mental picture of me haltingly walking into The Little Red Hen leaning on my walker. God's healing touch on my body had brought me a long way since then. I thought about how our friendship had grown into a beautiful one since we met there.

With tears in my eyes and a heart overflowing, I pointed upward to the heavens, giving God the praise and the glory for being able to do this relay. We serve an amazing God indeed!

I had gone from my hospital bed to a wheelchair to walking in the Sawtooth Relay—a definite milepost to remember. I felt it was a miracle of healing in my body that enabled me to complete this relay. I had experienced so much healing, physically, emotionally, and spiritually, and I was so grateful.

Marathon Spirit

It's not whether you get knocked down; it's whether you get up.
—Vince Lombardi

When I do the best I can with what I have, then I have won my race.
—Jay Foonberg, 72-year-old runner

HMM, THIS GAL IS going to be "interesting," I thought when I first met Brenda during an organizational team meeting for the Sawtooth Relay of 2011. But Brenda (Evers) Brown quickly became one of my best friends. My original impression was, *I am not sure I like this gal.* She was blonde, beautiful, athletic, determined, competent, and very organized—a take-charge kind of woman.

We as women can be judgmental and feel threatened by other women. We often initially judge each other like judging a book by its cover. I know there are lots of times when I need to let down my own insecurities and let the book—or the woman—speak for herself.

With Brenda I learned I simply needed to allow God to do whatever it was that He wanted to do with our friendship. Had I not allowed Him to drive the friendship, and put my own insecurities aside, I would have missed out on a powerful blessing.

When the time for the race came and we were traveling together in a Suburban, then having a meal and one glass of wine, I quickly realized Brenda was and is a wonderful woman. I would classify her as a W.W.W.O.G.—a Wild Wonderful Woman of God! We talked and shared throughout the sixty miles. I had passed judgment way too quickly! I really liked this feisty blonde woman with her nose piercing.

After the Sawtooth Relay, I so enjoyed her go-get-em spirit and saw what a strong and fast walker she was, and we became weekly walking partners. Every week we would meet three to four times at the Snake River Canyon to walk between three to six miles at a time on the Centennial Grade. Brenda soon became my favorite walking partner and one of my best friends. Every time we would meet to walk we would talk about our boys.

Brenda's Jax is the same age as my oldest son, David; her older son Justice is a year older. Her two daughters are grown and on their own. We'd talk about the challenges of life, work, and our church life. We soon became each other's "sounding board." With no other adults in my home, besides my adult golden retriever, Quinn, who is not a very good conversationalist, Brenda became the one I could talk to about anything.

One evening as we were walking, she mentioned she had done several marathons before and was contemplating attempting another one in September 2011.

Wow, I thought, that is 26.2 miles—that's a lot of fast-walking! I had done a couple of half marathons, 13.1 miles, prior to my car accident. But a marathon is twice that length.

I kept thinking about this and then prayed about it. The next time we met I said, "Brenda, I might like to join you on that marathon."

"Really?" she said, sounding surprised.

I went for it, researched online the Top of Utah marathon in Logan, Utah, and registered.

Emailing Brenda, I said, "I'm in for the marathon."

I didn't know it, but she was not even certain *she* was going to do that marathon. Once I had committed, Brenda felt like she needed to do this with me.

From July to September we trained for the full marathon. We even coerced one of my friends, Brenda's niece, Angie Hawkins, to go with us as our support person for the 26.2-mile trek. Angie would be the one who would bring us energy bars, bananas, coconut water, or whatever we might need during the marathon.

We trained, we planned, we prayed. We took care of all the details of having our families and children squared away so we could participate in the marathon. It meant a weekend away for three mothers who had a total of seven children at home for which they were responsible—no easy feat!

The night before the marathon we took the day off work and drove down to Logan, a four-hour trip from Twin Falls. We checked into our hotel and then headed out to a pre-marathon dinner at the Beehive, a quaint little restaurant. I had learned from doing races to eat whatever my body feels like eating that is healthy and will nourish me prior to a race. Instead of "carbo loading" and eating a lot of pasta, I chose grilled chicken, a salad, and some grilled vegetables. After we laughed and enjoyed our dinner, we headed back to the hotel to attempt to get some rest.

Sleep is often challenging before a big race. I was so excited and apprehensive and concerned about how my body was going to function and perform that it was hard to sleep. And I had a tinge of the what-if-I don't-hear-my-alarm fear as well. It was like not sleeping well the night before a flight because of worrying about missing the alarm and plane.

That Saturday morning when I woke up, I realized I had just got my period. And, of course, it was the heaviest flow; the worst timing for sure. Fortunately, I had packed provisions, hoping I would not have to use them. So, on top of making sure I was carrying water, energy blocks, my Garmin to track my pace and time, a baseball hat, and all the gear I needed to take with me for a 26.2, mile race, I had to include my feminine supplies—what a joy and a privilege!

At five in the morning, it was dark when we hopped on the marathon transport bus with lots of other animated participants. I sat beside a guy who liked to hear himself talk about how many marathons he had run. He was a member of a group called Marathon Maniacs, a group of folks who go all over the country doing multiple marathons in a weekend or a couple days.

As he chattered on about his accomplishments, I thought, *Here I am just trying to do my first marathon after recovering from my accident and eight surgeries.*

Long before he stopped chattering, my mind had switched gears to the challenge before me. I would be walking my first-ever marathon. As I looked around at the others on the packed bus, I wondered about the story each one could tell of how they got to this place. *What motivates them? What compels them to go 26.2 miles?*

That distance was just a little bit shorter than the distance from my parents' house in Farmville to my grandparents' house in Amelia. As the bus made its way through the winding roads and out into the Cache Valley of Utah where the race would start, I thought about how as a child and teenager that ride going to my grandparents seemed like an eternity in the car. Now I was setting out to walk almost the same distance.

When the bus stopped, Brenda and I made our way to the massive "starter" tent packed with excited racers all huddled together before the big race.

We met a delightful woman who had just completed the St. George, Utah marathon.

And then there were the two middle-aged sisters dressed alike in matching pink shirts and shorts. After losing their mom to breast cancer several years earlier, they were doing the marathon in her honor. The sisters had each other to do their memory walk of purpose with—walking and talking and remembering their mom. *What a beautiful thing*, I thought.

Just before the race was to start we heard raindrops on the top of the tent. Then it began to absolutely pour, a torrential downpour. I looked at Brenda and she looked at me and said, "Come rain or shine, sweetie, we are doing this thing."

What next? I wondered.

But that's the way it is with races and marathons. You sign up months in advance, you train, you shave time off your miles, and then race day you can't be a "fair weather" racer.

We were committed to see the race through and finish well—just like the Bible tells us: "Run with endurance the race that is set before us" (Hebrews 12:1).

At the starting gate, we were like stampeding cattle when the race megaphone went off. I was off and walking fast through the gorgeous hills and valleys of the Cache Valley.

At the risk of giving you too much information, the first five miles I had to stop to attend to myself at each mile port-a-potty. I was bleeding profusely and the intensity of the exercise caused the bleeding to be even more intense.

I knew my stopping was holding Brenda up and causing us to not go as fast as we would normally go in a race. But she was a trooper, and was incredibly kind and full of grace to hang in there with me.

At about mile twelve it started pouring rain again.

Then the thunder and lightning started.

"Brenda, have they ever pulled people from a marathon because of weather?"

"I've never been in a race where that happened."

By that time, it wasn't just raining, it was a torrential deluge—a pelting and soaking rain. We were soaked to the bone. The weight of the water in our soaked shoes made walking fast difficult and frustrating. It was like trying to walk with eight-pound weights in your shoes.

We had texted Angie to meet us at milepost 17 with dry clothes and shoes as well as plastic ponchos to protect us from the elements. When we arrived at our designated meeting place, we couldn't find her. "Where's Angie?" I asked, looking around, by then completely soaked and miserable.

There was nothing to do but keep going, while we kept trying to contact Angie. We continued to trudge along the race route, the whole time trying to locate her and wondering what happened to her.

The course had taken us out of the Cache Valley and was now routed through a neighborhood. As we trudged along the residential streets looking for any sign of Angie, I thought about how famished I was and how I longed for a banana, dry clothes, and shoes.

Up ahead I saw a blonde woman walking in front of us carrying some plastic bags.

"How odd," I laughed and said to Brenda, "Who would be carrying bags in a race?"

When we caught up to the blonde woman we realized it was Angie! Our precious support person was the strange lady on the course.

"Angie," Brenda said, laughing. "We wondered why this strange woman was carrying bags on the course."

"I couldn't find you," said Angie, obviously stressed, "so I parked my car and started walking." Somehow, we had gotten our meeting place mixed up or it was not well marked.

Angie had a blister on her foot because she had been walking along searching for us wearing the wrong kind of shoes.

She led us to where she had parked and we got in the car and started peeling off our wet clothes and shoes and putting on dry ones as fast as two five-year-old girls wanting to get into dress-up clothes. The clock was ticking and we needed to get changed and back on the course as quickly as possible so we could finish.

"Thank you, Angie!" we waved as we hit the race trail again in our blue plastic ponchos at mile 19. We would meet Angie again at the city park where the race would end.

Only 7.2 miles left to go! We had added on some time by stopping and changing clothes and shoes, but I am not sure that we would have made it in our drenched clothes and shoes.

Those last six miles were my hardest of the whole race. I was exhausted and my body needed rest. The only thing to do was press on as hard as I could toward the finish. I was listening to music on my iPod Shuffle, hoping the music would motivate me and get my mind off how tired my legs felt. I had to push through. But for some crazy reason the iPod Shuffle kept getting stuck, so I listened to the *same* two songs for about the last four miles!

The last two miles felt like the longest two miles ever. *I'll never get to the end*, I groaned. By then we were in in the middle of downtown Logan, walking past storefronts.

As we approached the marathon finish line the rain stopped and the sun came out. It was as if God was smiling down on us.

I did it! I had actually completed a marathon—despite a horrific time of the month, rain, wind, thunder, and lightning. I hadn't run it, as I am a walker. I hadn't made a winning time. But I had completed a marathon! I had persevered! I felt tired, but incredibly grateful and amazed.

Someone placed a gorgeous race medal around my neck. I looked over and there was Angie waiting for us. We changed out of our tennis shoes into slip-on shoes to give our feet a rest, and headed over to the free massage tables they had set up for the finishers. Brenda and I both found an open table and relaxed as the therapist worked some kinks out of our weary bodies. It felt glorious to have someone massage my sore and tired body.

Angie took our pictures, complete with medals and smiles. "Who's going to get the bathtub first to soak?" I asked as we made our way to the car. At the hotel, we had Epsom salt baths, rested, and then dressed for a celebratory dinner back at the Beehive, our new favorite restaurant in Logan. We chatted and laughed and shared—and it was a wonderful time. I was so grateful for friendship, partnership, and for Brenda's belief in me that I could finish; and for Angie, our faithful support person.

What a phenomenal day! I was grateful to the Lord for giving me the strength to complete the marathon. I had never done a marathon before my accident, but now, after all I had gone through, I could add this to the milepost achievements I was thanking God for.

I wondered about the others on the bus to the race. Did they all finish? Did anyone get sick or injured along the way? Did they make their goals? I was sure there were many stories out there. I had only one story: Brenda and I had completed the Top of Utah 2011 Marathon and I had a medal to prove it!

Romans 5:4 tells us suffering produces perseverance, character, and hope. It had been a day of suffering and perseverance, but I knew that my character had been strengthened and my hope renewed. *To God be the glory, great things He has done!*

Scars Like Jesus

Scars have the strange power to remind us that our past is real.
—Cormac McCarthy, *All the Pretty Horses*

Out of suffering have emerged the strongest souls; the most massive characters are seared with scars.

—Kahlil Gibran

AS A WOMAN, MY legs have always been important to me. I want them smooth, soft, shapely, with muscular calves. I guess we women are like that because we want to be attractive to the man in our lives who loves us. Or, if you are like me and currently do not have a significant other, you might want your legs to be attractive so the man who may not have found you yet will like your legs.

Prior to the accident, I had decent-looking legs. Most folks in my family said I had my dad's legs. His are thin, "in shape" legs with a definite shape to the calves.

I tried to keep myself healthy by working out and lifting weights so my calves had some element of definition. Fast-walking for exercise since high school had helped tone my legs. But I didn't dwell on what my legs looked like until their appearance was dramatically changed by my car accident. Then I began obsessing about my legs.

It's not that my identity as a woman was wrapped up in my legs, but God did make us with them! I know legs are important to men. Men like to see women in pretty sundresses, long and lean, in business suits with skirts, in pumps or sexy shoes. Men like women in shorts and capris. Legs are a part of the total package that God created in woman. That is just the way it is.

Because of my accident, the appearance of my legs has been considerably altered. Whole sections of my legs were severely damaged. The wound vacs had to help grow skin back from the inside out. The skin grafts helped to make my legs look like legs on the outside and also enabled them to function properly. But the seven surgeries to my legs, along with the seventy-one staples from the skin grafts, had produced scars on the outside of my legs.

For almost a full year, I had to wear a black boot as part of the healing on my right leg. Once this accessory, and the wheelchair, and cane were no longer a part of my daily wardrobe, I was left with my two scarred legs.

Don't get me wrong; I am very grateful the Lord spared my legs. I am so glad I have them. But damage had been done to that part of my body. I found myself grieving what I had lost. Then I had to come to terms with how I was going to live with the results. *Can I be comfortable in my new skin?* I wondered.

I firmly believe the Lord only gives us what we can handle. He knew having a leg amputated would have been extremely difficult for me. I am eternally thankful that He chose to spare my legs.

I will never wear a dress or skirt or shorts again, I told myself. I figured if I'd just wear long pants then I wouldn't have to deal with folks asking questions like, "What happened?"

Wearing only long pants wasn't too realistic. So I tried wearing shorts and skirts and planned what I was going to tell folks when they asked. Initially, I'd used humor to see where that got me.

One day I was out in shorts and a lady who I did not know said, "Honey, what happened to your legs?"

Here goes.

"Actually, I was attacked by a shark. You know like the movie *Soul Surfer*?"

The woman gasped and said, "That's awful! Where did this happen?"

"At Red Fish Lake." That was a lake in Idaho north of the town we live in.

From the look on her face it seemed as if the lady was trying to comprehend what I said. Then she realized my story could not be true. "Now, honey, tell me what really happened."

"Actually, it was a piranha attack."

After a few moments, I told her the real story of my car accident.

As time went on and more folks asked, my story got a little bit easier to tell, and I gave up the comic relief opening. But I still felt frustration and irritation when I had to explain to people how I got the scars on my legs.

This went on until the Christmas of 2008, the first Christmas after I was divorced and the first holiday I would not have my kids with me. I had gotten counsel from both my DivorceCare group and other friends that it would be healthy to plan a place to go for my first holiday alone.

Where shall I go, Lord? I prayed.

The thought came to contact some dear friends, J.C. and Jody Anderson, and their daughter Katie Grace, in Nashville, Tennessee who I had been friends with for over twenty years, to ask about spending Christmas with them. Katie Grace is like a niece to me, so I knew she would help me not miss my kids too much.

The Andersons were very welcoming and invited me to come, so I booked a flight and headed to Nashville to have a Tennessee Christmas. I sensed it was important to me to be with others who loved me unconditionally.

Nashville is a wonderful place for the holidays, with Christmas concerts and all types of special music events taking place. I had hoped to visit the church where Jason Houser led worship. He is the founder of SEEDS Family Worship ministries and I had heard him perform at my church.

After we attended Jody and J.C.'s Baptist Christmas Eve service we headed over to Jason's church. I knew that with his caliber of talent and heart for the Lord that the music and service would be phenomenal. However, I was not quite prepared for how the Lord would meet me that night.

When Jason began to sing Chris Rice's song, "Welcome to Our World," I felt the Lord's touch. I had heard this song probably fifty times before this night, however, this particular time the lyrics went straight to my heart. *I took in every word as a healing balm to my soul.* The song talks about the coming of Jesus, the perfect Son of God who had to "wrap our injured flesh" around Him to be one of us. The powerful words of the song seemed to deeply speak to and transform my heart.

The healing words of the song went deep into my heart. I sat quietly and wept as the Lord ministered to me through the words "injured flesh."

I felt as if the Lord was saying to me, *Page, the scars on your legs are scars like Jesus had. You have scars like Jesus. When folks ask you what happened and how the scars got there, you get to tell them about me, and the story of your accident, and how I spared your life.*

As I sat still and quiet, the Lord reminded me of 1 Peter 3:15: "But in your hearts set apart Jesus as Lord. Always be prepared to give an answer to everyone who asks you to give the reason for the hope that you have. But do this with gentleness and respect."

The Lord completely changed my perspective on my scars with His words to me during that precious time of Christmas worship.

I have a scar on my right hip, just like Jesus had them on His sides. I have a scar on my right hand where metal pierced my skin and created a scar. On my legs, I have many scars. Jesus had many scars on His feet where the nails were hammered through to keep Him on the cross.

God had taken me all the way to Nashville for Christmas that year to be with my dear friends who ministered to me greatly that season. There He showed me one of the purposes of my scars. They are to bring glory to Him! I had reached yet another milepost of healing in being able to accept my scars.

My scars had a new meaning. They didn't look as ugly to me anymore. They had purpose, perfect purpose, a holy purpose.

Blindsided

Blindsided: to surprise or shock someone in a very unpleasant way.

"PAGE, I WANT YOU to know you are under investigation," the human resources director said.

"What? Why?" I said, totally confused.

I had just returned from a national conference for Safe Kids Worldwide in Washington, DC in June 2015. I was then the director of Safe Kids Magic Valley and had been the injury prevention coordinator for almost nine years. It was a wonderful position where I helped educate families and the community about the importance of wearing seat belts, bike helmets, etc.

When my boss scheduled a meeting with me on my first day back at work I thought it was just our monthly meeting to go over schedules and programs. My coworker Carma and I were to go together to the main hospital for this meeting. At the last minute, Carma said, "I'm going to drive separately."

That's odd. I wonder why she wants to do that.

When I got to my boss's office Carma wasn't there. My boss stood and said, "Our meeting has been changed to another room." I followed her down the hall to the human resources director's office.

As we walked into the HR office, I did not have a good feeling at all. My body started to shake and my mind went to the worst. *Are they going to let me go? I need this job.*

"Please sit down," the director said, not smiling. "Page, you have been written up twice in the past for offending two different people. Now you have just been written up a third time."

I tried to remain calm as I searched my mind for what could possibly have happened. The HR director continued, "Someone complained that you made some remarks that made them feel uncomfortable. We need to investigate this third accusation. This person says your comment about their religion made it uncomfortable for them to be around their office. They have had to close their door because they are uncomfortable."

I sat there feeling numb. *What? Who could have accused me of this?* It was like a bad dream.

"Could I please see the paperwork so I'll know what I am being accused of?"

"Absolutely not! You do not deserve to see any paperwork." The director's voice sounded as if he was on a power trip. I had heard about his ruthless behavior from other employees, but now I was experiencing it firsthand.

"You need to put your keys to the office on the desk, as well as your hospital badge. You are not allowed to talk to any other employees. Especially Carma. When we complete this investigation, you will get a call from us."

I did what I was told and walked out of the hospital in a daze, my body still trembling. *I can't believe this is happening to me.* I felt blindsided by my boss. I had trusted her. I was told to come to a meeting that I was not prepared for. Walking out of the hospital I was left with many questions and no answers.

Crying, I peeled out of the hospital parking lot feeling fragile and weak. I drove home worrying, *What if I lose my job? How can I provide for my boys and take care of myself? How can I tell my boys I might be losing my job?*

I never thought this could happen to me. I had been through a lot of different situations in life, but this was new territory. Overwhelmed with worry, I wondered *How long will the investigation take? When will they let me know?* I tried reading my Bible and praying, but I just couldn't settle down; there was no peace in my spirit. That night I cried myself to sleep.

The next day my phone rang. It was someone from the hospital asking me to come in at 1:00 p.m. for a meeting with my boss and the HR director.

That was quick, I thought. *Is the investigation done already?* I showed up at 1:00 p.m. that day and was told to report to the HR director's office again.

At the meeting the HR director said, "Based on our investigation we are going to have to ask you to leave your current position."

I just nodded and tried to come to terms with this devastating news. My stomach felt as if I had swallowed cement. I had never in my life lost a job before or been asked to leave a position.

"What about the personal stuff in my office?"

"You will meet your boss after hours at the Safe Kids office. She will make sure you only take the things that belong to you."

They obviously didn't trust me to leave with just the things that belonged to me. It all felt so awkward. *I can't believe this is happening to me.*

This job that I was passionate about and a program I had helped grow over the past nine years would no longer be mine. And on top of that, I would not have closure at all with the people with whom I had worked and built relationships with.

I wanted to say good bye to Carma and let her know how much I enjoyed working with her and her friendship over the years. We were a good team. She brought some amazing gifts to Safe Kids and I complemented them well. I thought we were a pretty dynamic duo.

That night at about 7:00 p.m. I met my now ex-boss and she watched as I packed up my belongings. It felt as if she was eager to help me get out of there as quickly as possible. She watched as I packed up my butterfly clock, my Mary Engelbreit artwork and collectibles, as well as the curtains I had had specifically made for my office to make it feel cozy and warm. Then she helped me carry things out to my car in boxes. Nine years of service and working to build a program was reduced to a couple of boxes of belongings.

As I got ready to get in my car, my ex-boss said, "It will be okay, kiddo. You will be fine. I'm sure you will find another job to go to." And then she moved toward me to give me a hug.

How awkward and weird. I thought, *Lady you have no idea how it will be.*

Losing my job meant I lost health insurance for me and my two sons. I was the sole provider for sons who were in high school and middle school. I did not have thousands of dollars saved up and had no idea how I was going to make it.

I knew my boss was very successful financially, she had a husband with a great job and profession, they lived in a gated community, and seemed to be "set" for life. How could she tell me it would be "fine"?

Resentment burned inside me.

It's not fine! I had lost my job. I had lost friends in the workplace who had become my family. Everything that seemed stable suddenly was completely unstable. *I am alone. How am I going to pay for my mortgage, food, gas, clothes, and activities for the boys? How am I going to be able to afford what we need to make a house a home?*

I was no longer in my known and stable world. Now I was in a new world and facing an unknown future.

The next day I drove to the Department of Labor to apply for unemployment. At the counter, I met Joe who was incredibly gracious to me and made applying for benefits easy. I was so grateful for him and how kindly he treated me as he walked me through the hoops I would need to jump through.

I began searching for jobs and put in applications. I knew I couldn't make ends meet on unemployment. *What am I going to do?* I knew I needed to supplement my income, but I couldn't earn too much or I would jeopardize the benefits.

Good friends Mary and Jim Fort asked me to help them with marketing for their photography business, so I worked for them for a few hours a week. When the county fair came along I worked in a food booth that Brent and Carla Reinke, a couple from our church, owned, along with some others from the church. I enjoyed working with folks who loved the Lord and also had fun while working.

I tried very hard to look at all the blessings during this time, and felt grateful for the little jobs that supplemented my income. Each week I searched for work in marketing and public relations, the field I am trained for and gifted in.

Then the husband of a Safe Kids board member called. "What would you think about coming to work in sales at my dealership?"

There is no way I can sell cars, I thought as I listened to his offer. I had no sales experience. The work sounded difficult, and I needed a regular check.

"Lord, is this a door you are opening?" I prayed. I sensed I was to just trust God, walk through this open door and see what happened.

I met with Dave, the owner of the dealership, and he convinced me to come to work for him. *Okay, I will try this sales gig for a bit and see what it's like.* Working on commission was scary. There was health insurance and I needed that for my boys. For a year I stuck with the car sales job while still looking for another job.

I heard of a position in advertising sales with a local company. After applying, I was called in for an interview with Desi. She seemed professional and kind and I liked her. More importantly, she seemed concerned about her sales team. It was evident she wanted them to be successful in their jobs.

When Desi offered me the job, I was so grateful because it came with excellent benefits and great growth potential. As a bonus, Desi has ended up being one of the best bosses I have ever had, and she has become a precious friend.

While I was getting started in my new job, I struggled to pay my mortgage and keep things going. *I have to do something. Maybe it's time to sell my home.* My realtor friend Sue helped me look at my finances and come to the decision to sell. The mortgage payment was too big and the house was too much for me and my youngest son, Champ to live in. I did not need a four-bedroom, three-and-one-half-bath house.

It was hard to think about selling the home where I had raised my kids. We had moved to Idaho and bought this house when Andrea was in fifth grade, David was four and a half and Champ was one and a half. The house was in a wonderful neighborhood, in a cul-de-sac with a park within walking distance. Our neighbors, especially Deb and Tony Haman, Lorraine and Dale Rapp, Amy and Tim Mingo, and Michelle and Steve Root, were like family. They had seen me through my accident and rehabilitation, and actually been more supportive than my own husband had been. These friends were some of the most supportive and caring folks I have ever met. We enjoyed spending time together. We'd block off the cul-de-sac and enjoy the long summer nights with cookouts and wine socials in the front yards.

I prayed and sensed the timing was right. This was the thing to do. In three years Champ would be in college and I would be home alone. I did not need this huge house to clean or to take care of. I felt peace about selling it, but also sad at what I was losing. I was selling my children's childhood home.

I needed to look at the positives as well. I could find a smaller place that would take less time to clean and maintain. This was my chance for a fresh start in maybe a new part of town. I'd start making new memories.

After months on the market, the house sold. I found a duplex across town and closer to my work. As I purged and sorted, sifting through my belongings acquired in fifteen years in the house, I remembered the hard and sad times in this house, as well as the happy times.

I looked around at the cozy den where my children and I had read books together and I had also watched unprecedented terror unfold during September 11, 2001. There was the kitchen table where they played with Play-Doh and did their homework. They had gotten ready for prom dates and homecoming dances in the bedrooms. I had baked soccer birthday cakes and brownies in the kitchen. The kids had built forts under the spiral staircase. Our house had provided an incredible place of solace and peace after my accident and during my rehabilitation.

Selling this home that my children had been raised in was yet another milepost, a change that was hard and difficult, yet seemed very necessary.

In our new life across town there would be new routes to school and work, and new neighbors. But God had led and directed and it was time to move.

The sale went through. I will never forget when the mortgage company sent me the final paperwork saying, "Your debt has been paid in full."

My debt was paid. I was free to step into my new life. Just like when Jesus paid our debt of sin on the cross and we could begin our new lives in Him.

The Big "C"

Then your light will break forth like the dawn, and your healing will quickly appear; then your righteousness will go before you, and the glory of the Lord will be your rear guard. Then you will call, and the Lord will answer; you will call for help, and he will say; here am I.

—Isaiah 58:8

I'M EXHAUSTED. IS THERE *something wrong with me?*

I had not been feeling well for a couple months. The extreme tiredness was not normal for me and I had noticed my tummy was bloated.

Despite feeling tired, I had been exercising a lot through the summer as I continued to train for my first 100-mile road-biking race.

After my birthday on September 3rd when I turned fifty-one, I realized I *should have had* a colonoscopy a year before on my fiftieth birthday, according to health screening recommendations.

Turning fifty the year before had been traumatic enough, so I had put off having my screening done then. As 2016 began to wind down I thought, *I'd better go ahead and get my colonoscopy done.* I had really felt prompted by the Holy Spirit to get this done, and besides, my insurance deductible was about to be met.

The soonest they could get me in and still be within the year was Wednesday, December 21. I followed the liquid, clear broth, Jell-O, diet a couple of days before the procedure and then drank the concoction that is part of the screening prep the night before the procedure.

Taking the day off work, I arranged for my dear friend Lawnie Kay to be my designated driver to and from the colonoscopy.

At St. Luke's I was given propofol, the anesthetic with the Michael Jackson connotation that knocks you out for the procedure. I knew a lot of the nurses who worked in Dr. Ward's office from when I was the injury prevention coordinator in the hospital for nine years.

Traci Hanson greeted me and explained how the procedure would go. I tried to relax and told myself, *This is just a screening; it'll all be fine.* Another nurse came in and hooked up my IV and I was quickly asleep. They are not kidding when they tell you it is "*the* best nap of a lifetime."

I woke up in recovery to see Lawnie's kind and attentive face.

"Dr. Ward will be in shortly to go over the results of the screening," a nurse said. I tried to adjust my hospital gown to make sure I was covered and tried to relax.

Dr. Ward came in the room and closed the door behind him. "I am so glad you came in for your screening," he said.

"I know, me too. That's off my list," I said, smiling. "Now I can focus on the rest of my Christmas preparations."

"No, I don't think you understand. I am *really* glad you came in. We found a mass," Dr. Ward said in a steady, yet concerned tone.

"Oh really? What do you mean by that? A polyp?"

"Actually, no. We found a mass that looks to be about five centimeters in circumference." He paused just slightly, then said, "It's cancer. You will need to have a CT scan as soon as possible to see if it has spread outside of the colon wall."

I didn't know what to say. The word cancer hit me in a way like nothing else has. *After everything else I've gone through. Cancer?*

Dr. Ward then showed me a color print picture of the inside of my colon. I could clearly see the mass. He said, "The mass is in the secum area of your colon. You will most likely need to have surgery soon to remove the cancer and that section of your colon."

As I looked at the picture my doctor was showing me it all became too real. *This is my body. I have cancer.*

It felt as if all the alarm systems in my body were on high alert, but I tried to take a deep breath and absorb everything the doctor was saying. I looked up at Lawnie and she too looked concerned and worried.

"If at all possible, I'd like to have the CT done *today* since I've taken the day off from work and I'm already here," I told Dr. Ward.

"I'll see if they can fit you in right away," he said and left the room.

I did not know it, but when he called radiology he got the head nurse, Mindy Renee. She had been a previous OB nurse when I was the car seat and SafeKids coordinator on the OB floor, so we had known each other for years. When she heard about the mass, she said, "I literally got sick to my stomach, worried about what the outcome would be."

Mindy moved patients around on the schedule like pieces on a crowded chessboard to make sure they could get me in immediately.

Once I was cleared to be transported to radiology, they whisked me down to the first floor for my CT prep. I am one of those rare folks who happen to be allergic to IVP dye. In a perfect scenario they would have given me prednisone prior to a CT scan. Because they could not give me the regular prednisone, they gave me a pretty heavy dose of Benadryl. This was precautionary to prevent any reaction to the IVP dye.

With the combination of the upsetting news of a cancer diagnosis I had just been given and the Benadryl, I guess I was quite animated and a bit loopy. I was laughing at myself and providing some entertainment for Jaime and Shanna and all the other nurses who knew me.

After the CT scan, I was released to go home. "Try not to worry," the nurse said. "Dr. Ward will call you with results of the tests as soon as he gets them, probably later this afternoon."

At home, I tried to rest and not think too much about what the last several hours had revealed. About 3:00 p.m. that day Dr. Ward called. Before I answered the phone, I took a couple of deep breaths to focus.

"Page, the CT shows the mass has *not* spread outside of the colon, or to the liver or kidneys. We will not know about the lymph nodes until we do the surgery."

"Ohhh." I said. That news was a bright spot in what now felt like a dark day.

"I'm going to refer you to Dr. Blair, the chief surgeon. His office will schedule the surgery for as soon as possible."

As I hung up the phone, a sense of gratefulness flushed through me. *Thank you, Lord!* The cancer had not spread outside the colon to the other organs. While grateful, I also thought about all the unknowns ahead. Until surgery was performed, I couldn't really know the outcome.

My son David was coming home from college that very afternoon. I had called and told him what they had discovered. He went right out and got his head shaved. When he came in the door with his newly bald head, he hugged me and said, "Mom, I did it for you. I want you to know I am supporting you."

That evening I didn't feel well—bloated, gassy, and uncomfortable. Both David and Champ were leaving the next day to go to their dad's in Boise for Christmas. I would only have that one night with them until they returned the week after Christmas.

"What do you guys want to do tonight?"

"Let's go to the movies," David said. So off we went to see *Office Christmas Party*. I don't think any of us wanted to think any more about the cancer diagnosis that night.

The next day at work I tried to act as normal as possible considering I had just found out I had cancer and would need surgery soon. I did not feel comfortable telling my coworkers so I just called my boss, Desi, to let her know so I could make the needed arrangements for taking time off work for the surgery and recuperation. Desi was amazing and understanding and really helped calm and comfort me. She assured me, "Don't worry about work. I'll be praying for the surgery to go well."

Prior to the diagnosis, I had planned to take a week of vacation after Christmas, but hadn't made any plans to go anywhere. The Lord was leading me even in arranging to take my vacation days.

My dear friend Michelle had invited me over for Christmas Eve dinner with her family and to accompany them to our Christmas Eve service at our church.

When I woke up on Christmas Eve, it had started snowing. White heavy flakes fell and covered the streets and fields much like a picture-perfect Christmas postcard.

Dressing warmly, I went out in the snow to walk and think and pray. Before I knew it, I had walked four miles. Alone, I talked to the Lord and tried to lay all my fears and concerns at Jesus' feet.

Feeling much better, I came home and showered and got ready to drive to Michelle's for dinner. By then it was snowing so hard and the roads were so bad that what would normally take me about twenty minutes took me close to forty-five minutes. She had prepared a beautiful table and delicious food and it was wonderful to be with her family. I wasn't alone. I could focus on the fellowship and not my fears.

We then all drove separately to Christmas Eve service at church. That night I was so glad to be surrounded by songs of hope and joy, celebrating the night before the birth of our Savior.

I awoke Christmas morning to a thick blanket of snow on the ground, a beautiful way to begin Christmas Day. I had slept in a little and then prepped the food I was to take to my friend Doris' home for dinner. She had graciously invited me to come and share Christmas with her family so I would not be alone.

We had a wonderful time eating and enjoying each other and the beautiful day. Her daughter Jessica and Jessica's husband Joe were both there. Jessica is an oncology nurse in Boise and I shared my colonoscopy pictures and report with her. I asked her some questions and voiced some of my fears and concerns about the colon cancer and the surgery.

When I got home that night I told the Lord, *You are so good. You gave me someone to talk to who really understands what I am going through.*

Ever since I heard I had cancer, my feeling was, *Get it out of me!* I felt very unsettled knowing I had something growing inside me that should not be there. I couldn't get it out of my mind that this could kill me if it wasn't removed properly and in the appropriate timeframe.

Tuesday, December 27 I had a follow-up appointment with Dr. Ward when he went over the CT results with me in person. He confirmed Dr. Blair, the chief of surgery with a specialty in laparoscopic surgery, would be the one doing the surgery.

My friend Shelley Bonnes, a nurse who knew Dr. Blair because she too had been one of his patients, graciously offered to go with me to my appointment on December 28. She would help me think through questions if I forgot to ask them. She met me at his office and we prayed together in his waiting room before we went in to see him.

Dr. Blair explained I would be having a colonectomy, which involved cutting a portion of my colon out and possibly some of my intestine. He would then reconnect sections of my colon to make it all function again. They hoped to get all the cancer by removing that section of my colon and the tumor. While they were in there for the surgery they would extract about twelve or more lymph nodes for testing as well. Then they would test the lymph nodes to see if they were at all cancerous.

"Dr. Blair," I said. "I'm concerned about missing a lot of work. I have this time off at Christmas and New Year's . . . and my deductible hasn't been met yet. Would it be possible for me to have the surgery before the end of the year?"

I rushed on. "I'm a single mom. And I'm in sales. When I don't work, I don't get paid. It's important to me to get back to work post-surgery as soon as possible."

Dr. Blair seemed to understand my predicament. He explained how I would need to prep for surgery, and then we followed him out to the scheduling and receptionist's desk.

"How would December 30 at 7:30 a.m. work for you?" he asked.

"Absolutely! The sooner the better," I said.

We made plans for Shelley to accompany me the day of the surgery. I needed someone to take me to the hospital and communicate with my family back East and my boys about how I was doing. And I was so thankful for her willingness to do this for me during her Christmas break. I just did not feel good about putting my twenty-year-old son in that position, especially if something were to go awry.

On Friday December 30, Shelley picked me up for the trip to the hospital. Again, she and I prayed together before I went under the anesthesia and into surgery and it felt good to do that.

After waking up groggy and a bit sore in recovery, I was wheeled to my room on the second floor. I was told the stapled incision above my belly button was only about two inches in length.

Shelley was there to greet me. She had brought me a beautiful Christmas-motif quilt stitched in reds, greens, and grays that was just the right size for a twin bed. She said her mother-in-law, Carla, had sent it to me and wanted me to use it in the hospital.

Alone in my room, I ran my hand over the bright Christmas quilt that made my sterile hospital room, my home for a few days, feel more like a decorated room in a cozy retreat center. I felt so grateful and so cared for by that beautiful gesture. *Thank you, Lord, for being with me, loving me, and showing me your care.* As I looked down at the quilt I thanked God for all the ways that He had seen me through some difficult days.

In the stillness of the moment I sensed He was saying, *Don't worry, Page. Don't you see I have this covered?* It was as if He was reminding me of how He had covered me in His love and the love of His people.

The next day I was starting to feel a little bit better, the catheter came out, and I could walk around more.

When Dr. Blair came by to give me a report on how the surgery had gone, he said, "I took out ten inches of your colon and the mass, as well as two inches of your intestine."

As I was absorbing that, he reassured me saying, "The cancer was stage 2A. It had not metastasized. It appears we got all of it." He went on to say he also biopsied seventeen lymph nodes. I had to wait for the results of those to come back from pathology.

Once he was inside, Dr. Blair saw my appendix was inflamed and took that out as well.

Feeling good about what my surgeon was telling me, I said, "The surgery was not that bad. I already feel so much better."

"Well, how you feel and heal is largely based on your attitude, and you have had a great attitude through all of this," Dr. Blair said kindly.

We were coming up on New Year's Eve and I was so grateful. I had a lot to be thankful for. The surgery had been done before the end of the year so my medical deductible could be met, and the cancer was only a stage 2A and had not metastasized.

A steady stream of my friends brought gifts and flowers to cheer me up in the hospital.

Those days in the hospital felt like a four-day church service. Christian friends and visitors and pastors came to see me and prayed for me for complete healing.

As my boys visited me each day I was grateful that they got to experience how God's people were living out being Jesus in the flesh.

Well, there's a first for everything, I thought. I'd never spent New Year's Eve in the hospital before. I've never been much of a partier or one to go out on the town to celebrate for New Year's Eve. I usually tried to stay safely at home where I'd reflect on the previous year and look forward to and pray for the year to come.

That night David hung out with me in the hospital. My son climbed on the bed with me and we both made some goals for 2017 and I wrote them down in my journal. After we had some good talks together, I told him, "Go home and celebrate." He was twenty years old and did not need to babysit his mom in the hospital.

I was exhausted and figured I would fall asleep well before the crystal ball dropped in Times Square.

The doctor had ordered a blood transfusion for my anemia as it had not really improved much at all. Because I had a transfusion after my car accident, my antigens were a bit off, which made matching the blood tricky. Because of a massive snowstorm, they were having a difficult time getting the blood from Boise. I never did have that transfusion but my blood counts improved anyway.

January 1, 2017, the first Sunday of the New Year, I felt better than the day before so I got up, showered, and got dressed in anticipation of visitors after church. I wanted to make sure I was looking my "hospital Sunday best." In my quiet time the day before I had read a quote that said, "God knows how to pack the good stuff into our day, our week, our year—even if our attitude gets a little wrinkled at times."

This unexpected colon cancer surgery had made my attitude a bit wrinkled. But, regardless of the cancer, the Lord was still packing good stuff into my life.

Janie Humphrey came to see me and showered me with gifts and a beautiful visit. As she sat down, she pulled out a journal, candle, a devotional, and an Ann Graham Lotz book, plus her special homemade caramels. We had made yet another full circle in our friendship. She had been the director of the transitional care unit at the hospital when I had my car accident. Nine years later, Janie was retired and visiting me as a dear friend.

Nurse Natasha came in and I reintroduced Janie to her. Nine years prior Natasha had been one of my favorite nurses during my stay after the accident. And now, she was my nurse for the weekend. Natasha got on the bed with me and posed for a picture that Janie took.

Monday morning came and I waited to see if my blood levels were high enough, and all systems were working, so I could be discharged. After lunch, I got the word and called my boys, David and Champ, and they came to get me. I needed help transporting all my flowers, gifts, and belongings. I was so ready to be home and to see my sweet little shih tzu/poodle mix, Ginger.

That morning my devotional quote for the day was, "Drive your cares to God, He loves you like crazy." I really didn't need reminding. I would never forget His words to me. *I don't need to worry, God, you've got my needs covered.*

That whole week we had a huge snowfall in Magic Valley, a record number of inches and the coldest temperatures since about the 1980s. The boys were good about shoveling it all while I rested, regained my strength, and tried to stay warm.

A small group of friends brought meals to the house. The boys loved that dose of homemade goodness. The last thing I wanted to do was stand up for long periods of time or cook, so all the meals were an answer to prayer. And my boys got to see the hands and feet of Jesus once again.

Waiting for the test results from the biopsies of my lymph nodes was hard. I called the first day they said they should be back but I missed Dr. Blair by seconds as he had left for surgery. Then we got another dump of snow, so much that his offices were closed the next day. No answer that day. By the end of the week I still did not know the results from the biopsies. I prayed and prayed that I would hear from my doctor on that Friday and not have to wait over the weekend to get the news.

Early Friday afternoon Dr. Blair called. As we began to talk, I sent up a quick silent prayer. *Lord, give me strength and grace for whatever the results might be.*

"So, I have the results from your lymph node biopsies and I am happy to report they came back clear. They are *not* cancerous," he said.

A deep joy and silent shout of *Hallelujah!* welled up inside me as he spoke.

"So, basically, what that means is the cancer has not spread? You got it all in the procedure?" My voice must have sounded a bit tentative. I think my doctor sensed a bit of doubt in my voice and my need for more clarification.

"Exactly," Dr. Blair responded.

"So, I will not have to undergo any chemotherapy or radiation at all."

"Correct."

A feeling of relief and reprieve and deep gratefulness to the Lord again came over me. My Lord had indeed covered me.

Dr. Blair went on to say the only other test I would need to have was a CT of my lungs to have a baseline and to make sure there were no spots of cancer on my lungs.

I got kind of a flu bug over that weekend and slept a lot and rested as much as possible. All the recommendations I read were to take two to four weeks off work after the type of surgery I had.

Thinking about my paycheck, I went back to work on January 9, fewer than ten days post-surgery. I had made the choice to go back full days instead of partial days and that was probably too much. I was tired, but I got through it.

On January 12, I went back to see Dr. Blair to have the staples removed from my abdomen after the laparoscopic surgery. I was so glad to have them gone.

I was back to work, so grateful to God for orchestrating my days, grateful that the cancer had been discovered so it could be dealt with, grateful that the surgery had gone well, that my lymph nodes had not been involved, and I was now cancer free!

The Longest Thirty-Three Days

Teach us to number our days, that we may gain a heart of wisdom.
—Psalm 90:12

GOING TO "CHURCH IN the woods" is what I call it on the occasions when I play hooky from attending regular Sunday services. January 15 was a beautiful Sunday to be out enjoying the Lord's creation. Just sixteen days post-surgery, Lori Satterfield White and I went snowshoeing up at Magic Mountain. I had wonderful memories of my boys learning to ski at this small, family oriented ski area.

As we walked through the heavy snow among the silent pine trees that looked as if someone had painted them with mounds of white cotton, I was thankful to be moving. I wasn't in a hospital bed; I was out enjoying nature. I wasn't feeling the effects of chemo; I was feeling fine, trusting the Lord for what was ahead.

January 19 I went to see Dr. Manning, my oncologist, for the first time. As I approached the hospital and saw the words, Mountain States Tumor Institute above the automatic doors, I thought, *This is one door I never imagined I'd be going through.*

Dr. Manning let me know that my "new normal" was coming for blood draws to MSTI every three months to monitor any rise in my numbers. For colon cancer, you want your CEA (carcinoembryonic antigen) levels to be less than or equal to three nanograms per milliliter CEA is a tumor marker for colon cancer. When it starts going up that can be an indication of cancer in the body.

The CT scan for my lungs was scheduled immediately after my appointment with Dr. Manning.

"I don't have any reason to believe we'll find any cancer on your lungs," he assured me, reminding me they needed to do this test for a baseline measure. Once again, I was wheeled to radiology for my CT lung scan.

As the radiology tech who was doing my procedure and I chatted, she shared with me that her mother had died of colon cancer two years prior. Her mom had lost her life to colon cancer!

As we talked, I felt so thankful my cancer had been found in the early stages and not when it was too late to do anything about it.

"You'll get a call with the results tomorrow," the nurse said as I left the hospital to go back to work.

I walked into my office just as the phone rang. My boss, Desi, excitedly said, "Open your email, Page!"

Opening the email, I started reading the letter from the president of our company. "Congratulations, you have made it to President's Club. Because of reaching your sales goals of over 101 percent you and a guest of your choice have won an all-expense-paid trip to Los Cabos, Mexico in March 2017. You will be receiving the details of the next steps very shortly via another email letter."

I knew that I had been doing well in sales, but I guess with the cancer diagnosis and operation, I hadn't tracked how high my sales numbers had been. While I knew about the possibility of winning this trip, I hadn't given it much thought.

Desi was so excited because she and two other coworkers were going as well, Brenda and Shellae.

It was a lot to absorb. I had recently returned to work after a major cancer surgery, and now had won my first-ever trip to a warm and gorgeous location. Feeling a bit overwhelmed, I left the office and headed home to share the news with my son Champ.

Too wound up to think about cooking, I called Champ and asked him, "What do you want me to pick up for dinner?"

"Panda Express is fine. The usual double orange chicken and chow mein," he said.

I pulled up in the Panda Express drive-through line, ordered, and then moved forward to the window to pay. As I pulled out my debit card, the gal at the window said, "The car in front of you just paid for your meal."

"Oh, thank you so much," I told her, as tears came to my eyes. *What a generous gesture of kindness.*

"Why are you crying? Folks don't usually cry when their food has been paid for," the worker said, smiling.

"I know . . . It has just been a big day. I just went through a colon cancer operation during the last month, had my last CT scan, and they are pretty sure they got it all. I found out less than an hour ago at work that I have won a trip to Los Cabos. And now this . . . Someone I don't even know paid for my food. It's all a bit overwhelming."

I pulled through the drive-through and found the car of the gal who had paid for my food. I wanted to thank her for her act of kindness. I knocked on her window and she hit the button to roll down the window.

"I just wanted to thank you for buying my food tonight. That was so very nice of you," I said.

"I don't normally do this, I usually do it at a coffee place, but tonight I just felt like I was supposed to pay it forward for you."

"Wow," I said, still feeling stunned. "You see I just went through colon cancer and it has been a hard month. Then today I found out I won an all-expense-paid trip to Mexico. And then I come here to get food for my son, and . . . you pay for my food."

"You just went through colon cancer? My mom died several months ago from colon cancer." The young woman looked at me with concern in her eyes. "I am so sorry. Are you going to be all right?"

"They think I'm cancer free, but I'm waiting for the results of the lung CT scan to come back."

We said good-bye and I drove home thinking about the goodness of God and the kindness of His people. As my friend Cappie would say, "You just cannot make this stuff up."

The next day at work I got a call with the result of my lung CT. It was negative. I was completely clear of cancer! I would not have to undergo chemo or radiation, hair loss, and other side effects. It had been exactly thirty-three days from diagnosis to the news that I was cancer free.

Thank you, Lord, for your mercy and hand on my life, I breathed silently.

That afternoon as I left work feeling light and full of joy, I thought, *I'm going to buy myself a "cancer free" gift to celebrate life*. I drove to a sporting goods store and bought a pair of snowshoes, poles, and a carrying bag. I was looking forward to spending more time in the cold and snowy winter months outdoors enjoying my life and gift of health.

Once I had regained my strength, a couple months after my cancer surgery, I began training again for my first "century" ride—100 miles. I was determined to do a century in June of that year. After registering online, I recruited some bike sisters to go with me to Utah and compete in my first century ride, the Little Red. In 2016, I had done the 50-miler on this same course, but this would be my first 100-miler.

I finished my first 100-mile bike ride on June 2, 2017 in Logan, Utah, just six months after my colon cancer surgery. Three weeks later I did my second century, the MS Harmon bike ride also in that same area of Utah. On July 22, I completed eighty-five miles of the Cycle Magic Valley bike ride.

On my birthday that year, I rode fifty-two miles to celebrate. God has given me more life to live and I want to live it to the fullest.

In the aftermath of my cancer surgery, I am using my voice to educate others about screenings as a colon cancer awareness spokesperson here in our community. As a living example, I've been interviewed on TV, and my local hospital featured me in an article as well. I have spoken at a cancer fundraiser and been a speaker at our local community college addressing the importance of screenings.

Today, a year later, I just had my yearly colon screening and am completely free of cancer! My screening and early detection of my cancer had saved my life.

Afterword

Then they cried to the Lord in their trouble, and he saved them from their distress. He sent out his word and healed them; he rescued them from the grave. Let them give thanks to the Lord for his unfailing love and his wonderful deeds for mankind.

—Psalm 107:19–21

I HAVE TOLD YOU my story.

You have read of the breaking of my protective shell through unrealistic expectations, anorexia, disappointments, and my life-altering accident at Milepost 95. You have read how I was emotionally abandoned in my marriage, and suffered job loss and a health crisis.

In my fifty-two years, I have come close to death three times: in 1986 when I almost starved myself to death when I had anorexia; then in 2007 with the wreck that not only caused physical injury, but lots of internal wreckage that resulted in the loss of my marriage and family as I knew it. And then in 2016 with a diagnosis of colon cancer that could have ended in a much different way.

God has brought me through the mileposts I have told you about. My days of being flat on my back or struggling through rehab brought me closer to God as I learned to depend on Him. God has worked deeply in my heart, my life, and my emotions through what I have gone through. I have leaned on His strength to become stronger and better, not bitter.

One thing I haven't yet told you about is the transition of my daughter, Andrea Nicole, to become my son Andrew Nicholas Geske. I have learned what it is to be the parent of an adult transgender child. God has shown me how to love and continues to teach me how to love unconditionally.

I was recently given a card saying, "Beautiful girl you were made to do hard things, so believe in yourself." It is God's strength that makes me strong . . . and the knowledge that I am His precious daughter—the daughter of a King.

My story is not your story, but if you find yourself struggling with unexpected or unwanted transitions in your life, I trust you will persevere as you lean into God who can also redeem your story into something beautiful.

My life almost ended at Milepost 95. But it didn't.

Since then God has faithfully taken me through each of the hard things I have gone through and given me back a richer, fuller life.

I thank the Lord Jesus Christ, my Lord and Savior, for the difficult things I have endured and for the strength to believe my story matters and my scars matter.

I believe we are put on earth for a purpose. We all have a destiny. Our stories matter to God and the ones around us. My prayer is that this book, which is an offering to the Lord, will bless you. If there is despair and discouragement in your life, may the Holy Spirit speak life and hope to you so you can share your own story of the mileposts where God has met you.

I welcome you to reach out to me via my website (www.milepost95.com), Facebook (Page Geske Author), or Instagram (Page Geske). As we are real, authentic, and intentional with each other and tell our stories, God heals our wounds just a little bit more.

Page Geske

Acknowledgments

I AM FOREVER GRATEFUL to all the people who have had an impact on my life. For those who have believed in me, and believed that my story matters, and that it would bless and inspire others.

Jesus Christ my Lord and Savior and to the Holy Spirit who constantly guide and encourage me on my journey of faith:

Thank you for all the ways you have wooed me to yourself, loved me with an everlasting love, spoken to me in quiet moments, or through your powerful word. You have always let me know I am not alone and that you have not and will not ever forsake me. You truly are the air that I breathe.

My children, Andrew, David, and Champion:

I pray from the depths of my soul that you will each know the deep love of Christ in real and tangible ways. May you be able to grasp the incredible purpose He has for each of you. May you truly know the only way to really be happy in this life on earth is to know Jesus personally as your Friend and Redeemer.

My parents, Marvin and Lee Scott:

I can never really put into words how grateful I am for you both. You have sacrificed a lot in life for me. Thank you for coming and taking care of me and my kids while I rehabilitated and gained my strength and health back after the wreck. Each of you in your own way has shown me deep, profound, and unconditional love, and I am forever grateful!

My sister, Anne Scott Meehan:

You have always been that faithful confidante in a little sister. Thank you for encouraging me to pursue my dream of writing my story to help others. Your belief in me and your support has been a lifeline. You are my sister and one of my best friends.

Margie Gillespie, Susan Anderson Wampler, Marsha Jordan, Rachel Matthews, Jody Anderson and Laura O'Connell Jacques:

Your friendship over the years and your example of living out what it means to love Jesus have been paramount in my life. Thanks for loving me when I was unlovable.

Prayer Warriors: Chris Smith, Michelle Frosthensen, Kay Wolverton, Sandy Flora, Sue Loosli, Donna Krueger, Leslie Grant McClure, Tina Phelan, Mo NiHill, Jim and Mary Fort, Kara Fort, Doris Daniels, Staci Mallet, Barbara Stoddard, Robin Porter, Carol Jones, Mary Shaw, Lawnie Kay and David Bolster, Kristi and Martin Anderson, Beth Miller, Kathy Taylor, Ana Marie Gierhart, Ellen Curtis and Lisa Jennett:

Thank you for all the many times you allowed me to send you group text prayers. They literally helped me get this book written and encouraged me to never give up and to have faith and trust the process.

Kara Fort:

I am grateful that a book on migraines and Mary and Jim Fort introducing us brought us together, but Jesus has been the glue of our friendship over six-plus years. Thanks for encouraging me to write, and for helping me to believe that my story does indeed matter. You were there in the beginning to help create and draft the first one-page synopsis. And then you have come full circle to be the cherry on a sundae by helping to do the final edits. You are a precious friend. Thank you for using your wordsmith gifts on *Milepost 95*. I will always be eternally grateful for your presence in my life.

Wendy K. Walters:

For believing in me and speaking prophetic words over me at Release the Writer 2017 in Oklahoma City, Oklahoma. You are indeed the first in my fellowship, and I accepted the ring and the challenge. Thank you for helping me to believe in a Sam and a band of brothers, a fellowship of the ring. You are a lifter and an accelerator and more importantly a launcher. I'm grateful that you have played a huge part in helping shoot me out of the cannon and into the final writing of this book.

Athena Dean Holtz, founder and publisher of Redemption Press:

Thanks for responding to my email when I reached out to you at Redemption Press. Your encouragement, confidence, and belief in me and the importance of telling my story helped catapult me into a contract with Redemption Press. My first publishing experience has been a great one. You and your staff have been godly, professional, and intentional in the publishing of this book. I thank you and am so very grateful.

Inger Logelin, senior editor at Redemption Press:

You have been such a gracious and kind editor for me and I am so very thankful. You have helped me craft and create meaningful sentences out of my broken story. Thanks for blessing my life during this time of writing my first book. God knew I needed you for such a time as this!

Christie Jones, my "book twin" and peacock sister:

I am so grateful that God allowed us to meet at Release the Writer, just when I needed you the most in my life. It has been an honor and a joy to be several steps behind you in the publishing of your first book, *A Vessel of Noble Use*. Thanks for spurring me on to the calling of writing that God has for me.

David, me, and Champ Geske, Christmas 2017 celebrating my
almost 1-year anniversary of being cancer free.

Doris Daniels and me hiking near Pioneer Cabin in October 2017.

Lee Warriner Scott, my precious mom who was my main caregiver after my accident in 2007.

Leslie Grant McClure and me at Champ's football game in the fall of 2017.

This is me on June 3rd, 2017, holding up my bike after I completed my first 100-mile Century Bike race, The Little Red in Logan, Utah.

Me and Dorothy Mitchell, my biking partner in crime for my Century.
Not pictured Beth Lamb

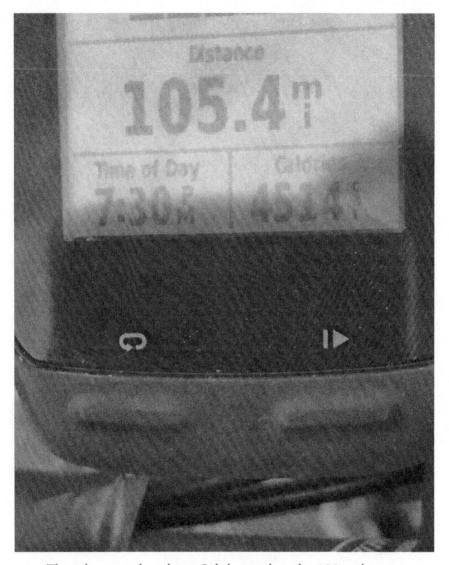

The odometer that shows I did complete the 100-mile race.

Me, Lynda Hawkes, and Tina Cobia, 2nd Century Ride, June 24, 2017 This was the MS Ride in Logan, Utah—my 2nd 100-mile Century ride.

Me, and my son, Andrew Nicholas Geske, October 2017. We had just taped an NPR interview on "Crossing Borders", a story that captures the reality of a parent and a transgender child's relationship at the NPR Boise State Radio Station. Interview done by Rhesa Ledbetter.

http://upr.org/.post/crossing-borders-mother-and-her-transgender-son-reflect

Family photograph L to R: my mom, Lee Warriner Scott, my sister, Anne Scott Meehan, me, and my dad, Marvin Wade Scott, August 2017 in front of the house I grew up in in Farmville, Virginia.

Marsha Brown Jordan, my best friend since college at Virginia Tech.

Photo Credit: Brayden A. Weeks, www.braydenaweeks.com. The actual Milepost 95 scene of the accident on a wintery day.

My wedding picture, June 11, 1994, The farmville Herald

Me, Leslie Grant McClure, and Carol Jones. Precious friends that have been present for many mileposts in my life.

Pioneer Cabin

Snowshoeing at Magic Mountain with Lori Rebecca Satterwhite, January 2017, a couple weeks after my colon cancer surgery.

2004 Honda Pilot at Milepost 95 right after the wreck on July 1, 2007.

Another shot at the scene with the emergency vehicles in the background, July 1, 2007

Me and Andrea, my daughter at the time and driver in the accident.

Me during the Sawtooth Relay 2009. Pointing to God and thanking Him for the strength He gave me to finish the race well.

Me and walking partner, Brenda Brown after we had completed the Top of Utah Marathon in September 2011.

Order Information

To order additional copies of this book, please visit
www.redemption-press.com.
Also available on Amazon.com and BarnesandNoble.com
Or by calling toll-free 1-844-2REDEEM.

CPSIA information can be obtained
at www.ICGtesting.com
Printed in the USA
LVOW03s1102060318
568792LV00004B/17/P